Manuals for Students of the Society for the Home Study of Holy Scripture and Church History

THE
TEACHING OF ST. PAUL

BY

BURTON SCOTT EASTON, D.D.

PROFESSOR OF THE INTERPRETATION AND LITERATURE OF
THE NEW TESTAMENT, GENERAL THEOLOGICAL
SEMINARY, NEW YORK

WIPF & STOCK · Eugene, Oregon

Wipf and Stock Publishers
199 W 8th Ave, Suite 3
Eugene, OR 97401

The Teaching of St. Paul
By Easton, Burton Scott
Softcover ISBN-13: 978-1-6667-3440-9
Hardcover ISBN-13: 978-1-6667-9021-4
eBook ISBN-13: 978-1-6667-9022-1
Publication date 8/23/2021
Previously published by Edwin S. Gorman, 1919

This edition is a scanned facsimile of
the original edition published in 1919.

CONTENTS

CHAPTER		PAGE
I	THE EPISTLE TO THE PHILIPPIANS	1
II	I THESSALONIANS	26
III	I CORINTHIANS 1–4	47
IV	I CORINTHIANS 5–7	69
V	I CORINTHIANS 8–11	96
VI	I CORINTHIANS 12–14	125
VII	I CORINTHIANS 15–16	147

BOOKS REQUIRED

FOR ALL COURSES

The Holy Bible, American Revised Version. A copy of the King James ("Authorized") Version should also be at hand for comparison.

The Apocrypha, Revised Version.

A Bible Atlas The maps in any good Teacher's Bible will generally be sufficient

A *Dictionary of the Bible,* Edited by James Hastings. One Volume Edition. New York: Charles Scribner's Sons. 1909.

A large note book, substantially bound

A good Bible Concordance is recommended, but it is not indispensable.

FOR THIS COURSE

The New Testament: A New Translation By James Moffatt New York: George H. Doran Company.

METHOD OF WORK

The Directions given in the Studies should be followed exactly, sentence by sentence, and, in particular, *every* Biblical reference should be looked up and verified The important part of the course is the written work in the note book; ten minutes spent in writing is usually more profitable than an hour spent in reading. The note book is to be submitted at the close of the course, before the student can be admitted to examination, and it must contain all written work directed in the Lessons, and (as far as possible) the answers to *all* the questions asked. These answers should never be given as a simple "Yes" or "No"; they should include the wording of the question and give reasons for the reply E g , if the question reads, "Did St. Paul visit Neapolis?" the answer should take the general form, "Acts 16. 11 shows that St. Paul visited Neapolis." If a question seems too difficult, do not hesitate to say so frankly, but never leave a blank

When the review of a Study is directed, a review of the corresponding part of the note book is always to be included.

The direction " Illustrate " occurs with considerable frequency; this always calls for written work, some-

METHOD OF WORK

time rather at length. Subjects taken from modern life usually form the best illustrations. "Explain" is to be treated similarly. "Note" or "Observe" may be given briefer comment, but something should always be written.

DEVOTIONAL APPLICATION

Each Study should be begun with the Collect for the Second Sunday in Advent At the close a short extempore prayer, gathering up the main thoughts of the Study, is preferable to a formal Collect

As the note book is to be submitted for examination, it should not contain intimately personal matter, and for this reason the questions in the Studies avoid direct reference to the experiences of individual students But the possibility of such personal application will constantly be apparent, and it should be watched for. A second note book may be kept for devotional purposes, and keeping it may prove the most profitable part of the course. The Studies have purposely been made a little brief in order to allow time for this aspect of the study.

DIVISION OF TIME

The course presupposes an hour's study each day, but it has naturally been impossible to make all the Studies the same length. When extra time is given to some, others may be shortened, provided the average of one hour is maintained Sometimes it has become necessary to combine two or three Studies for a subject that does not admit of an easy division; in this case the total of two or three hours may be arranged according to the student's convenience.

If the Studies are found too long, the illustrations, etc., may be condensed. But directions to look up or copy out passages should never be neglected

FURTHER STUDY

Students may be able to complete Studies in less than an hour, or may be able to devote an average of more than an hour each day to study. Such students should work through the regular Studies, until the end of a Section is reached. At this point will be found lists of books and references for a more detailed investigation of the material covered. These books should be procured in advance, to avoid delay when they are needed, but they should not be used before the proper time; a rather full knowledge of the text of Holy Scripture should always precede the use of commentaries.

SECTION I

THE EPISTLE TO THE PHILIPPIANS

1

Note carefully the following facts · — Philippians was written during St. Paul's imprisonment, in Rome, at a time when he was expecting a decision about his fate. It is a letter to a dearly beloved congregation. In part it is a letter of thanks for a substantial gift sent him by the readers, in part it is a letter giving personal news, in part it is an exhortation to unity, and in part it is an exhortation against evil influences. Copy these points.

Now read the Epistle through as a continuous whole. Reread it, observing the portions corresponding to the above.

2

Find Philippi in a Bible Atlas. Note that it lies about nine miles from the seacoast, and that its seaport is Neapolis. With the atlas still open read Acts 16.8–12, verifying all the geographical references. The date of this trip (part of St. Paul's Second Missionary Journey) was about the late spring of 50 A. D.

Read the rest of Acts 16 and summarize the whole chapter in writing.

In the Dictionary look up Troas, Samothrace, Neapolis, Philippi, and write the principal facts regarding each place. In modern times the site of Philippi is wholly uninhabited.

3

In the Dictionary read the article, "Philippians, Epistle to" Look up all the Biblical references, and note in writing the chief points.

Reread the Epistle as a continuous whole.

4

1 : 1–11

Read vv 1–2 Note how St. Paul puts his young assistant, St. Timothy, on an equality with himself. In the Dictionary read the article "Holiness" rapidly, and explain (in writing) the meaning of "saints" in the present passage. The fundamental idea is, "The Christian is 'different'" "Bishops and deacons" need not detain us here The greeting in v. 2 is almost invariable in St. Paul's Epistles; explain it

Read vv. 3–11, observing that "the day of Christ" is the Day of Judgment. Note the three terms "furtherance," "defence," "confirmation," used with "gospel" How do these three terms define all missionary effort? The readers are "saints," but are they perfect (vv 6, 9)? Explain the optimism of v 7.

THE EPISTLE TO THE PHILIPPIANS 3

Compare the Revised version with Moffatt's translation, and note the principal differences in writing What changes seem a special improvement? Do any seem to alter the sense? Are there any you dislike? (In subsequent lessons these directions and questions will be summarized in the formula "compare Moffatt's version.")

In the Dictionary read the article "Grace," with especial attention to Section 3

5
1 : 12–18

Read these verses. In the Dictionary read the article "Praetorium," which states one theory of the meaning in v. 13 A more probable theory is that which understands "Praetorian Court," the tribunal before which St. Paul was tried Interpret v 13 in this sense, showing how it would explain St Paul's hopefulness

Does St. Paul complain of his imprisonment? Why not? Read St Mark 13 · 9–13 and show how it bears on this section But St Paul's attitude is no easy going optimism; God turns apparent evil into opportunity for good, but man must use this opportunity. Illustrate.

vv. 15–17 are interesting: were Apostolic Christians much better than those of today? The meaning in v 15 is, "They are so jealous that they preach more energetically, to counteract my fame." Does the difference between St. Paul and these preachers have theological importance (v. 18)? Explain how personal jealousy could arise. How does v 18 define the true characteristics of spiritual leadership?

Compare Moffatt's version.

Paraphrase the section in your own words.

6

1 : 19–26

Read these verses. St Paul's trial was drawing near, and it might result in a sentence to death. How does he balance the probabilities? Note that vv. 19–20 are unconcerned with the issue; he only hopes to make a showing worthy of Christ's Apostle. Paraphrase these two verses, so as to make the meaning clearer. "Live" in v. 21 appears to be more general than in v 22; explain the difference.

Note the strong social sense displayed in this section; exemplified in the appeal for prayer in v. 19, and in the motive in v. 25. Write a brief note on "spiritual unselfishness," illustrating. In v. 26 the "glorying" is the success of missionary effort. This should be the sole boast of any church. What are some common violations of this principle?

Compare Moffatt's version. He uses italics to designate an Old Testament quotation, here Job 13 : 16 (compare it). Why is "release" in v. 19 unsatisfactory? His version of v 26 is rather individualistic.

THE EPISTLE TO THE PHILIPPIANS

7
1:27–2:4

There is no break between the chapters; read these verses as a continuous whole.

The tendency of all groups of people is to form factions, and this was perhaps the greatest temptation in Philippi So note the insistence on "one" in 1:27 and 2:3. What is meant by "doing nothing through faction or vain glory" in 2:3 (illustrate)? How does a "manner of life worthy of the gospel" (1:27) contrast with this? Reread the whole passage, and call attention to further applications of the two questions just asked

1:28–30 contains a little digression. Fear of persecution might lead to mutual mistrust or recrimination; illustrate. In v. 28 "which" refers to the first clause; "your being unfrightened proves that they are wrong and you are right" Explain this more fully; genuine trust in God gives calm confidence. How could this principle be abused? v. 29 develops the thought further; suffering on behalf of Christ is an "imitation of Christ," which should make the sufferer happy in its promise of good results. Explain. And, as St. Paul was rejoicing in copying Christ (vv. 12ff), the Philippians could rejoice in copying St Paul (v. 30). State vv. 28–30 in your own words.

The "suffering" in Philippi was not danger of martyrdom or (probably) of legal action in any form. Men were abusing the Church, sneering at its ideals, cutting off social intercourse with its members, etc. How are such conditions (more subtly) paralleled today? How should such attacks be regarded? Compare Moffatt's version.

8

Review of 1:1–2:4

Reread these verses as a continuous whole. Then, from memory, make a written outline of their contents. Correct and supplement the outline from the Bible. If sufficient time remains, repeat the process.

(These instructions are always to be followed when the review of a Biblical passage is directed.)

9

2:5–11

This is one of St. Paul's "great" paragraphs. But note carefully that it occurs naturally in the Epistle, and that it is a vital part of the argument; since Christ humbled Himself, we should be willing to humble ourselves, so as to avoid factions. Read 1:27–2:11 as a continuous whole, and observe the smoothness of the connection. Reread the passage in Moffatt's version, which is not essentially different; if there seems to be any real divergence, study both versions until the reason for the change is clear.

Much needless difficulty in vv 6–11 could have been avoided, if interpreters had observed that St. Paul

THE EPISTLE TO THE PHILIPPIANS

writes from the *human* standpoint, which defines God primarily as "He who is worshipped." Before the Incarnation, Christ, although divine, lacked "equality with God" in this sense; men did not worship Him explicitly. Explain the meaning of the passage as thus understood. A quite different interpretation will be found on p. 691 of the Dictionary (column 2); state it in your own terms. Still a third will be found on p. 707 of the Dictionary (column 2); state this also in your own terms. Compare the three interpretations and explain the differences between them. State which seems the best, and why.

10

Review Study 9. Note particularly that, a widespread opinion to the contrary notwithstanding, the "Name" in which "every knee shall bow" is not "Jesus." The new Name was not given until the Ascension, and it consequently is "Lord." In this title men now recognize His "equality with God."

Copy the following passages: — Acts 2:36, Romans 10:9, I Corinthians 12:3, II Corinthians 4:5, I St. Peter 3:15, Revelation 19:16, Philippians 2:11. What element is common to them all? Do they seem to contain a primitive creed? Which passages point most in this direction?

The essential point in the title "Lord" is an immediate, personal relation between Christ and the world; He is in heaven, but He is here also, to guide and control all things. (Copy this definition.) Copy Ro-

8 THE TEACHINGS OF ST. PAUL

mans 14:9. So it is by this title He is addressed in prayer; copy Acts 7:59, II Corinthians 12:8, Revelation 21:20, I Corinthians 16:22 (with the margin).

So to say "Jesus is Lord" is to say "Jesus rules the world" Why was this the ideal first Christian creed? (Note that the Jews and many Gentiles already believed in God)

11

Review Study 10 Read Acts 2:22-36, 3:12-26, and the comment on these passages in the Dictionary, p. 705. In these speeches what does St. Peter say about Christ? What does he leave unsaid of the contents of Philippians 2:5-11? Do these two speeches in Acts contain as much about Our Lord as we believe today? What is missing?

Is there any reason to suppose that on Pentecost St. Peter already understood the full significance of all the facts about Christ's Person? Would it be natural to expect that even he would need time to appreciate their full meaning? Does the fact that Philippians represents more matured reflection than these early speeches add or detract from its importance? (But note, The Church has always held that true revelation ceased with the Apostolic age).

Even in St. Paul there are passages in which the undeveloped language is mixed with the more developed; in the Dictionary read carefully the last paragraph of III, 4 on p. 708, and summarize it in writing.

12

In Acts 2:36 note that "Christ" and "Lord" are used as two different terms, remember that "Christ" is only the Greek form of "Messiah."

Read Acts 3:13–21 (observing that "the Lord" in v. 19 means the Father). Does this passage say anything about the *present* activities of Jesus? Copy Acts 10:42, 17·31, II Corinthians 5:10 (contrasting the use of "Lord" in vv. 6, 8). What distinction do these passages suggest between "Christ" and "Lord"?

Properly, then, "Messiah" meant "the author of judgment and the bringer of final salvation"; as Messiah, Jesus' work looks towards the future, as Lord it looks towards the present. Note how in Philippians 2:11 "Lord" is added to "Christ" as a further title, denoting a further office. What, then, is involved in the phrase, "The Lord Jesus Christ" (explain fully)?

But this strict use of "Christ" soon became obsolete. Reread Philippians 1, and observe that the original meaning occurs only twice (where?) Otherwise the title has the same force as "Lord," which it tends to replace. What is the modern use?

13

Apostolic thought could not long remain content, even with the two titles "Messiah" and "Lord." He who had such rank could not be a mere human being, whom God exalted, He must always have been

10   THE TEACHINGS OF ST. PAUL

of divine nature   Explain the necessity of this reasoning (can anyone *become* divine?)

Copy Romans 8:3, I Corinthians 10:3-4, II Corinthians 8:9, Galatians 4:4-5, Colossians 1:16-17. What do these passages add to the results of Studies 10-12? Note that in none of these passages does St. Paul argue, he makes his statements as matters of fact which everyone accepts. Does this point to a very early and rapid acknowledgment of the truth of the doctrine implied?

For representative passages outside of St Paul copy Hebrews 1:2-3, I St. Peter 1:11, I St. John 1:1, Revelation 1 17   What do they teach about Our Lord? How do they agree with St Paul's doctrine?

In the Dictionary read the article " Logos " rapidly.

14

Review Studies 10-13, and write a paper on the development of the Apostolic doctrine about Our Lord, from the terms " Christ " and " Lord " to " Logos."

15

2:12-18

Read 1:27-2:18 as a continuous whole. How is the appeal summarized in 2:12-18?

In v 12 why does St. Paul say " much more in my absence "? Name and illustrate the virtue alluded to. " Work out your own salvation " does not mean " try to be saved "; it means " complete your part in the work God is doing for you " What is the difference in these interpretations?

How does v. 13 explain the " fear and trembling " of v 12? How do vv 14–15 condemn peevishness in the spiritual life? Illustrate the principle What is the missionary emphasis in these verses? Is the Church today living up to St Paul's exhortations (state the good as well as the evil) ? The faults of the Church are the faults of her children; where can laymen help in remedying these faults (be concrete)?

In vv. 16–18 note St. Paul's entire unselfishness. State the principle involved, generalize it, and illustrate it as a duty today. In what sense is " Christ " used in v. 16?

Compare Moffatt's version. In vv. 15–18 he does not give the missionary emphasis; is this an improvement or otherwise?

16

2: 19–30

Read vv. 19–24 Note St. Paul's driving zeal, whch cannot conceive that any one should neglect work for the Church. A journey from Rome to Philippi was a very serious and expensive matter; does the complaint in v 21 seem exaggerated? Note the good in such zealous enthusiasm What are its drawbacks? How does the magnitude of the task justify St Paul's high praise of St. Timothy? St. Timothy is much more than a mere messenger; what is he expected to

12 THE TEACHINGS OF ST. PAUL

do in Philippi? Note the tact of St. Paul's recommendation.

Read 4:18, and then read vv. 25–30 here. The Philippians had sent Epaphroditus to act as assistant to St. Paul, but he was taken seriously ill, and the attack was followed by despondency and homesickness. (Is such a sequel to illness common? Illustrate.) St. Paul does not dare keep him any longer, but does not wish to have the Philippians think he is a deserter. Again note the tact of the language In the Dictionary read the article "Epaphroditus."

How does this section illustrate St. Paul's power of personal affection? Note that this affection has no sentimentality about it; its objects have earned it through their services to Christ Generalize this principle and illustrate.

Compare Moffatt's version.

17

Review of 2:5–30

(Cf. Study 8)

18

3:1–16 (1)

This is a difficult passage to modern readers. Read it through. The kernel is the word "flesh" in vv. 3–4. Now compare Moffatt's version. Note that he renders "flesh" by "outward privilege," which gives the sense fairly well; how are "flesh" and "outward privilege" connected?

Jews laid stress on their possession of God's Law, the keeping of which would lead to salavation. Read Romans 2: 17–20 and Psalm 147: 19–20; how do these passages bear on the discussion? The Jews, consequently, thought salvation was a matter of personal achievement; what is objectionable in this conception? Read II Corinthians 12: 5–10; how does this passage bear on the discussion? Copy Romans 3: 27. Read St. Luke 18: 9–14; does the Pharisee "glory in the flesh"? Read the parable again and insert Philippians 3: 5–6 after v. 12; are not these verses an admirable continuation?

To "glory in the flesh," accordingly, is to boast of one's achievements in some narrow theological sect or system. Instance some modern examples More broadly, such glorying occurs where anyone boasts of personal achievements in the spiritual life. How does St. Paul safeguard himself in vv. 13–14?

19

3: 1–16 (2)

Read St. Mark 10: 13–16 When a father presents a gift to his child, does the little one normally argue about having earned it? A child wishes to please its father; does this wish normally proceed from a desire for reward? Define the childlike attitude in this sense. Transfer it to the spiritual realm, and contrast the childlike attitude with the Pharisaic attitude.

When St Paul uses " faith " he (generally) does not mean " belief that Christ exists," but " trust in Christ, as a child trusts its father." Does such faith lessen the desire to please Him by good works? Why not? Does it lead us to claim salvation because of those works?

With this preparation, write an explanation of St. Paul's famous phrase, " justification by faith."

Note that this doctrine is very easy to understand through the analogy of a child's attitude towards its father, Our Lord's figure But it is very difficult to define in rigorous intellectual terms. Many elaborate treatises on justification only serve to confuse, and St Paul himself sometimes grows obscure when he undertakes to analyze justification more closely. For instance, read Romans 5: 12–21, but do not spend much time on this passage.

20

In the Dictionary read the article " Justification," but do not spend more than an hour in studying it

21

3. 1–16 (3)

Review Studies 19–20, and observe how v. 9 sums up the whole doctrine of justification

Read vv. 5–7 The more a man is led to trust in

himself, the less he is apt to trust in God; illustrate How does this explain the word "loss" in v. 7?

Note that St Paul had no objection to observing the Jewish Law, when such observance meant merely conforming to local customs. Read I Corinthians 7: 18–19, 9· 20, Acts 21· 17–26 Read also Romans 14: 1–5 for his attitude in some matters that were purely "ritual" He fully realized that ceremonies may be a great help to devotion; how is this seen in the passages just read? His objections arose only when such ceremonies were held to bring salvation of themselves, or that their observance is necessary to salvation. Then they are a "loss" (explain why). Such is the point in the present argument, which is directed against those who sought to terrify the Philippians into accepting the Jewish Law

Read v. 2, and look up "dog" in the Dictionary. The word was used by Jews to describe Gentiles (St Mark 7: 27–28), and St Paul turns it against the Jews. What was his justification? "Concision" means "mutilation," and decries physical circumcision as a mere mangling of the flesh; the rare word is used because of its similarity to "circumcision" (Moffatt's "incision" is perhaps better) Copy Romans 2: 28–29.

State the argument in vv 2–9 in your own words.

22

3: 1–16 (4)

v. 10 introduces a new thought. In justification the believer commits himself to Christ, with the desire (St. Paul now adds) to become like Christ. This is obviously an indispensable ideal in Christianity. Hence the believer must be willing to suffer, as Christ did, even to die, as Christ did. (Note. Do not bring in here the thought of Christ's death as an Atonement; we cannot share in that) A Christian, consequently, should realize that suffering, disappointment, and apparent defeat may all belong to the path we tread with Christ. Cf. 1: 29–30 and the notes on these two verses.

But note St Paul's order in v. 10; the resurrection stands before the suffering. If sufferings are to contribute to salvation, power from the risen Christ must first give the needed strength. Explain and illustrate; may not suffering make a man worse instead of better?

In v. 12 St. Paul returns to the main argument. *Two* are concerned in salvation; we strive to lay hold on the risen Christ *because* He has already laid hold on us. State this in more theological language. In v. 13 "the things that are behind" are those enumerated in vv. 4–6. How can this principle be generalized?

State the argument in vv. 10–14 in your own language.

THE EPISTLE TO THE PHILIPPIANS 17

vv. 15-16 add a gentle little postscript. "Perhaps some of you think I am too uncompromising in my doctrine. Never mind; keep on patiently, and time will show that I am right." (Moffatt's version is very clear.) Note this very human touch.

23

3: 1-16 (5)

One phrase in this section remains for further consideration, a phrase found also in earlier parts of the Epistle. Copy 1:1, 1:13, 1:26, 2:1, 3:14, 4:7, 4:19, 4:21 (Do not include 2:5). In all of these passages underline "in Christ." Add 3:9a to this list, underlining "in him."

"In Christ" is one of St Paul's most loved phrases; it is rarely found outside his writings, and he may have coined it. It is explained most fully in Romans 6:1-11 and 8:1-11; read these passages and copy Galatians 3:26-29, II Corinthians 5:17.

These references make clear that "in Christ" means "in union with Christ," the bond of union being the Holy Spirit. Christ is in heaven, and believers are on earth. But the two are not separated, for the Holy Spirit carries the life of Christ continually into the soul of the believer. Illustrate this more fully from Romans 8:1-11. State this fundamental truth in your own words.

Returning to Philippians, the meaning of 2:1 (for example) may be expressed thus:—"If our union with Christ gives us any power of exhortation," etc. In the list written at the beginning of this Study expand all the other passages similarly.

24

Review of 3: 1–16

(Cf. Study 8)

25

3: 17–4: 1

Read this section 3: 1–16 is directed against Jewish agitators, but here an entirely different class of men is meant. In the Apostolic age, as now, men might think membership in the Church sufficient, without moral effort How are such men described in v. 19? Explain each clause separately (to "glory in their shame" is to glory in things of which they ought to be ashamed; illustrate). Why are such people "enemies of the cross of Christ" (v. 18)? Has Christianity any worse foes? But does the occasional presence of such men in the Church at all invalidate her claims?

The translation of vv. 20–21 in the King James Version is notoriously obscure. Read it, and explain in detail why the Revised Version is preferable.

The contrast in vv 20–21 is with the "earthly things" of v. 19. We cannot help having a "body of humiliation" during our earthly life, but we can

THE EPISTLE TO THE PHILIPPIANS

avoid yielding to its temptations. But what is our final hope? Note the assuredness in v 17. St. Paul knows that he is not perfect (vv 12–13), but he knows that he is making good progress To him this is simply the language of natural dignity, but should lesser men use it? Yet should not everyone who is "in Christ" be able to use it to some extent?

Compare Moffatt's version.

26

4: 2–7

Read vv. 2–3. We know nothing of the persons named in this section: the identification of "Clement" with St. Clement of Rome is reckless. Probably there are four names, for "Yokefellow" is a proper name ("Synzygos") St. Paul plays with its meaning, "Thou art rightly called 'Yokefellow'," just as we might say, "She is rightly called 'Grace'"; explain. For the "book of life" compare Psalm 69: 28, Revelation 20: 12–15 How literally is the idea to be taken?

Read vv. 4–7 Note the sequence "rejoice,— be not anxious,— pray,— so ye will have peace." Generalize this as a rule for personal life. The so called "Christian Science" body has proved that this rule is entirely practicable, even under modern conditions Suggest some practical means for a more general realization of its truth.

v. 4 What is the meaning of "in the Lord"? Can there be any greater reason to rejoice? In v. 5

the word translated "forbearance" is hard to render; "gentleness" may give the sense better. A joyful spirit never tends to be overbearing; illustrate. Does v. 6 contain a practical recipe against worry? Of course no one can live up to it always (compare II Corinthians 7:5), but it represents an essential ideal of our religion.

No words are more familiar than those of v. 7, but do we think enough of their meaning?

Compare Moffatt's version.

27

4:8-9

Read these verses It is very possible that v 8 is a quotation from a Greek philosopher; cf. Acts 17:28. Even inspired writers are not above using the good they find in non-Christian sources; generalize and illustrate the principle involved Cf. Romans 2:14-15; how does it apply?

v. 8 should be committed to memory. Whatever its origin, nothing can be more specifically Christian in its emphasis on the *positive* side of the spiritual life. Instead of saying "avoid evil thoughts" St. Paul says "keep the mind filled with good." The Ten Commandments are mainly a list of prohibitions; contrast Our Lord's method in St. Matthew 7:12, 22:34-40. Here are two ideals of religion; on the one hand, that of personal sinlessness, on the other that of active social benevolence. Illustrate them in their most extreme forms and contrast them. Are they wholly incompatible in less extreme forms? What is the proper balance?

Read St. Matthew 12:43-45. How can this be interpreted to explain the failure of merely negative virtue?

Compare Moffatt's version. (To American ears "high-toned" is a most unfortunate rendition; "well-approved" gives the meaning.)

28

4:10-23 (1)

This passage contains St Paul's thanks for a gift of money carried to him by Epaphroditus. Read these verses.

The presentation of a donation of this sort to a sensitive and highly spiritual man is always a delicate matter; illustrate. But in St. Paul's case there were special complications. Read I Corinthians 9:1-18, without spending too much time on the details, II Corinthians 11:7-12, 12:12-15, I Thessalonians 2:9. What was St. Paul's usual rule about accepting money? Why did he make this rule? What traits in his character does this show? Can he properly be described as "sensitive" (1:17, 2:21)? What traces are there in the present passage of this sensitiveness? Does it lead him, perhaps, to a slight ungraciousness here? Would such sensitiveness be at all incompatible with a power of intense affection?

Would it be apt to make him some enemies? How would they describe this feature of his character? Is such sensitiveness necessarily a vice? Is its absence always desirable?

Sum up this aspect of St Paul's character in your own words; no one has ever claimed that he was *perfect,* so do not be afraid of criticizing a little.

29

4:10–23 (2)

Reread the passage as a whole, and review Study 28. Note the tact of the sudden self-correction in v. 10; explain it Why does he introduce vv 11–13? Note how vv. 14–20 strive to make up for the slight ungraciousness in vv 11–13 In v. 14 " well " is not strong enough; " ye did beautifully " is the literal translation In v. 15 " the beginning of the gospel " means the beginning of St. Paul's work in Greece Compare II Corinthians 11:8–9, and show the application Does II Corinthians 11:8 indicate that St. Paul accepted occasional gifts from outside Greece? In v. 18 he succeeds in overcoming his reserve. Why does v 19 follow from v. 18? In v. 19 explain the force of " in Christ Jesus."

In v. 22 " Caesar's household " denotes the vast retinue of the Emperor's palace; look up the phrase in the Dictionary The Christians in this " household " probably had a congregation of their own. Why would St. Paul be brought into especial contact

THE EPISTLE TO THE PHILIPPIANS 23

with this group? Compare 1:14 (one interpretation).

Note the simple dignified close, and its freedom from sentimentality.

Compare Moffatt's version.

30

Review of 3·17–4:23

(Cf. Study 8)

31–32

Review of Studies 1–30

Spend these two hours in going over your notes, and in reviewing the more important matters

33

Review of the Epistle

(Cf Study 8)

34

Answer the following questions from memory: —

1. What was the original meaning of "Christ"?

2 What was the original meaning of "Lord"? Why was not God the Son "Lord" before the Incarnation?

3. What is the meaning of "in Christ"? How is it related to the doctrine of the Holy Spirit?

4. What relation has being "in Christ" to the

imitation of Christ? In especial, how does it give value to suffering for Christ?

After answering these questions, correct and expand your answers from your notes.

35

With the aid of your notes, try to answer this question as fully as possible: — What did the doctrine of Christ do for St. Paul and for his converts? Consider the assurance of forgiveness, the possession of spiritual power, the assured hope for the future, the amendment of life in the present, the creation of relations with one another in Christ, the sense of the Church's social responsibility to the world Apply all this to the present day.

FOR FURTHER STUDY

The following commentaries will be found most useful: —

The New Century Bible (published by Frowde). Philippians is in the volume entitled *Ephesians, etc ,* by G Currie Martin. The volumes in this series are all excellent, even if brief.

The Expositor's Bible (published by Doran, and inexpensive). The volume on Philippians is by Robert Rainy. A little old fashioned, but useful practically.

Sadler's Commentary is rather out of date, but will often be found helpful.

The Philippian Gospel, by W G. Jordan (Revell). An interesting practical exposition.

Paul's Joy in Christ, by A. T. Robertson. The most recent of all (1917) Vivid, but occasionally undignified.

One or more of these commentaries may be compared with the work done in the Studies, all differences being carefully noted in writing. The student should endeavor to form an independent judgment as to the preference in such cases

In the Dictionary the articles " Messiah," and " Paul the Apostle " will repay the most careful study.

SECTION II

I THESSALONIANS

36

Note carefully the following facts: — I Thessalonians was written from Corinth, during St. Paul's Second Missionary Journey. It is a letter to a congregation who had been converted from heathenism only a few months previously. St. Paul had heard that enemies were trying to shake the faith of these neo-converts, and he was naturally much worried about them. Consequently, he had sent St. Timothy to Thessalonica, to warn the congregation, and to bring him news. The latter rejoined St. Paul at Corinth and brought a splendid report. So St. Paul immediately wrote this Epistle, voicing his profound relief.

Copy these points in writing.

Now read the Epistle through, as a continuous whole. Note particularly that 3:6 gives the immediate occasion of writing.

37

Review Study 2, briefly. Find Thessalonica in a Bible atlas, noting that it is the Saloniki of fame in

I THESSALONIANS

the Great War, and that it lies about 80 miles from Philippi. With the atlas still open read Acts 17:1. In the Dictionary look up Amphipolis, Apollonia, and Thessalonica, and write down the principal facts regarding each place

Read Acts 17:1–9. Observe that, while St. Luke speaks only of a three weeks' ministry to the Jews, he does not exclude a much longer stay (after v. 3). In v. 4 "devout" is a technical term, meaning "regularly attending at synagogue worship"; cf Acts 13:43. In the Dictionary read the article "Proselyte."

Note that in Thessalonica the opposition to St. Paul came largely from the Jews; contrast the case in Philippi.

38

With the atlas open read Acts 17:10–18:1 (do not spend too much time on the speech in Athens). Note especially 17:13, and compare it with 17:15. The animosity of the Thessalonian Jews was evidently intense. In the Dictionary read the articles on Beroea, Athens and Corinth; in the case of Corinth note down the facts rather fully.

Read Acts 18:1–18, and look up Cenchreae in the Dictionary.

Acts 18:12 probably gives us a close date, for there is good evidence that Gallio became pro-consul about July of the year 51 Hence v. 11 dates St. Paul's arrival in Corinth towards the beginning of 50 A. D., so that his stay in Thessalonica belongs in the year 49.

Sum up the events after St Paul left Thessalonica.

In the Dictionary read the article, "Thessalonians, First Epistle to," noting down the chief points, and looking up all the Biblical references.

Reread the Epistle as a continuous whole.

40

1:1

Read this verse "Silvanus" is simply another form of the name "Silas" in Acts He first appears in Acts 15:22; copy this verse. Read Acts 15:36–41, copying verse 40. Note Acts 16:19, 25, 29, 17:4, 10 Copy Acts 17:14–15, 18:5. In the Dictionary read the article "Silas."

Read Acts 16:1–3, comparing it with II St. Timothy 1:5. St. Timothy was evidently a much younger man than St. Silas; cf. Acts 15:22 and note the order of the names in the present verse. In the Dictionary read the article "Timothy."

Note that this Epistle is addressed to "the *church* of the Thessalonians," contrast Philippians 1.1. There is no special reason for the difference Christianity did not introduce the word "church" (*ecclesia*); it was in current use among the Jews. In the Dictionary read the article "Congregation," and note down the chief facts. How does St Paul indicate that this church is Christian? Explain the meaning of "in Christ"

I THESSALONIANS

41

1 : 2–10 (1)

Remembering that the Epistle is in part a letter of thanksgiving for good news, read these verses. The style may seem a little confusing. St Paul dictated his Epistles to a stenographer (shorthand was widely practiced in the ancient world); does anything here suggest conversational style? Note that vv 3–9 each contain at least one reason for St Paul's thanksgiving; make a full list of them all. Does there seem to be any attempt at systematic arrangement, or is the order that of free conversation?

Cf v 2 with Philippians 1·3. To be named in St. Paul's prayers must have been a great privilege! St Paul tells of speaking to God before he speaks directly to the Thessalonians; why?

v. 3 gives the great triad of Christian virtues, each with an attribute, explain the appropriateness. Is there any distinction between "work" and "labor"? (Moffatt's version makes a rather arbitrary difference.) For the effect of hope, "patience" is too weak, why is the marginal variant an improvement? What is the meaning of "in Christ" in this connection?

42

1·2–10 (2)

Libraries have been written on the word "election" (v. 4), but St. Paul does not use it here in any profound sense; his readers were mere beginners in Christianity. But read the article "Election" in the Dictionary. How much of the doctrine stated can be assumed here?

The "power" of v. 5 was ability to convert; explain. What does "and in the Holy Spirit" add? From 2:3 explain the meaning of "assurance." With v. 6 cf. Philippians 1:30, 3:17, 4:9; why did the presence of false teachers make this warning important? Why is not "affliction with joy" self-contradictory? In v. 7 explain Achaia.

"The best argument for Christianity should be the lives of Christians" (vv. 7-8); explain. Note the vigorous "sounded forth." St. Paul exaggerates a little, no doubt, but the facts themselves were the Thessalonians' highest praise. Is the thought of personal holiness as a means for converting others sufficiently emphasized nowadays?

Note that, while a Jew might have written v. 9, v. 10 is almost a little creed. Note "Son" as a title of Christ; it was not used in Philippians. Here it *need* not mean more than "Messiah."

Compare Moffatt's version.

43

2:1-12 (1)

St. Paul's enemies attacked his character viciously, accusing him of error, guile, covetousness, flattery, etc. Why were such charges made? What effect might they have on the Thessalonians? Was contradicting them a mere matter of pride, or was an important duty involved? Read the section, noting that "we" often means St. Paul alone (v. 18).

Where in Acts is the "shameful treatment" of v. 2 described, and what was its nature? The "conflict" is probably the opposition of the Jews from Philippi (references?), but the word may mean simply "anxiety" In v. 3 "uncleanness" is used in the sense of "worldly motives."

Why in v. 4 is St. Paul's sense of responsibility so tremendous? Does not every Christian share it to some degree? In v 5 "a cloak of covetousness" might better be rendered "cloaked covetousness"; explain. Why the distinction between "ye know" and "God is witness"?

Explain the "religious democracy" in v. 6, noting however, that St. Paul's authority was real, and that he was often obliged to use it. In v 7 the figure is rather marred by the addition of "own"; explain. Why is it introduced (cf. Galatians 4:19, I Corinthians 4:15)? What is meant by "imparting our own souls" in v. 8?

Compare Moffatt's version of vv. 1-8.

44

2:1-12 (2)

Review Study 43, and reread the whole section Review Study 28. In v. 9 how does St. Paul's labor refute the charges of covetousness in v 5 and of "seeking glory" in v. 6?

With v. 10 St Paul begins to sum up. What is the distinction between "holily," "righteously," and "unblamably"? With v. 11 cf. v. 7. St. Paul's earnestness leads him into repetition Why is the figure here better than in v 7? Note that with v 12 St. Paul ends with an exhortation on the highest plane.

Compare Moffatt's version of vv. 9–12.

State the argument of vv. 1–12 in your own words. Explain the passage as depicting an ideal missionary. How is it also the ideal of any layman?

45

2: 13–16

Read these verses, noting that they resume the praise of the readers from chapter 1. Does v. 13 add anything new, or is it a recapitulation?

vv. 14–16 are perhaps the sharpest denunciation in all of St Paul's writings. He had had extraordinary difficulty with the Jews in Greece (how did this appear in Studies 37–38?), and even Philippians 3:2 is less savage But note how the denunciation has a true religious and moral basis; "contrary to all men" in v. 15 is explained in v 16 Is this basis sufficient to justify the denunciation? To "fill up their sins" rests on the idea that sinners may be punished by being abandoned to sin more Is this a fact? Explain

I THESSALONIANS

and illustrate. Cf. Genesis 15:16, and show how this verse applies.

Compare this denunciation with Our Lord's arraignment of the Pharisees in St. Matthew 23 (read it rapidly, but note v 32 especially; why?). Sentimentality towards reckless sinners can do the very greatest harm, illustrate. When can flaming anger become a Christian virtue? Distinguish this from selfish personal passion.

For a calmer attitude of St Paul towards Jews read Romans 9:1–4, 10.1–2; what is the difference?

Note that Gentiles as well as Jews were persecuting Christians (v. 1) But the Jews were the instigators

Compare Moffatt's version.

46

Review of 1·2–2:16

(Cf Study 8)

47

2:17–3:13 (1)

St. Paul now turns to matters of personal news. Read this section as far as 3:11. A few months earlier St Paul had not known a single Thessalonian; describe briefly the vitality of the religion that had given him such affection for these former strangers. What passages in Philippians does v. 17 recall?

The conception of Satan as the author of extraordinary human trials goes back at least to the Book of Job (glance at chapters 1–2). Cf. II Corinthians 12:7. Might not St. Paul have said with equal truth, "It was not God's will that I should come?" (cf. 3:11). How can the apparent divergence be reconciled? In the Dictionary read the article "Satan" (do not spend much time on it).

Note the perfect simplicity and beauty of vv. 19–20.

Review Study 40, as far as it relates to St. Timothy. Compare his movements noted there with those in vv. 2 and 6 of chapter 3. How much is left unexplained? (That matter has not enough importance to warrant much study.) Did St Luke intend that Acts should contain a full record of St. Timothy's travels?

48

2:17–3:13 (2)

Review Study 47. With vv. 3–4 (of chapter 3) cf. Philippians 3:10. In suffering or affliction men are sometimes tempted to say, "There is no God"; why? What is our reply? But St Paul knows the difficulty of always keeping the Christian doctrine in mind; note the gentleness of vv. 2–5. And observe how greatly he had been worried (vv. 1, 7), in addition to his own troubles in Corinth.

Why is v. 8 a perfect thanksgiving? The last clause of v. 10 is not meant to be a reproach; explain it.

Compare Moffatt's version of 2:17–3:10. Is his

change of "we" to "I" an improvement? In 3:6 is "kindly" satisfactory?

Read 3:11–13, and compare Moffatt's version.
Summarize 2·17–3:13 from memory.
Reread chapters 1–3 as a continuous whole

49

4:1–7

St Paul now passes to a discussion of special topics; read these verses Note the "Finally"; why is it much too early? Cf. Philippians 3:1. Does the fact the Epistles were dictated explain this rhetorical error?

Note the tact of v. 1. It is a reproof, but the readers are addressed as men anxious to do their best; explain. Is this a good model for reproofs? Note "in the Lord," and explain it

In v. 2 the plural, "charges," (as in the margin) is correct; vv. 1–2 introduce everything in vv. 3–12 How many "charges" do vv 3–12 contain? "Through the Lord" is curious English; it means "through the Lord's inspiration," "on the authority of the Lord."

In treating delicate subjects St. Paul always uses simple, direct language; is not this method much the wisest? "Vessel" in v. 4 may mean "body" or it may mean "wife" (cf II St. Timothy 2:20–21); scholars are unable to decide. Explain the meaning of the passage in each sense. Is there any particular difference in meaning? Which sense do you prefer (give your reasons)? The dominant thought in these verses is given classic expression in I Corinthians 6: 19–20; state it in your own language. How does "the Lord is an avenger" comport with modern tendencies to ridicule or condone laxity in marriage?

St Paul speaks only of the husband's duties; how much of his language is applicable to the wife also?

Compare Moffatt's version The quotation in v. 6 is from Psalm 79·6 (verify it).

50

4: 9–12

Read these verses "Love of the brethren" here probably means especially "see to the support of the poor." St Paul's laudation is especially high, but there is always room for greater effort, note "abound more and more," and cf. 3·12. Again note St. Paul's tact; the praise leads gently to the " But " in v. 10.

vv. 11–12 deserve special study. Christianity does not mean idle dreaming, it should be a stimulus to fidelity in this world's tasks. The possession of high ideals does not make common duties less necessary; explain and illustrate. Note the excellent marginal alternative for "study", is it an improvement? Is there not a little irony in "be ambitious to be quiet"? What fault is reproved here? How might sudden conversion to Christianity tend to make the convert the reverse of "quiet"? "Do your own business" means "work at your own profession," which should

I THESSALONIANS

absorb all of one's surplus energy. Among St. Paul's converts this "profession" was generally a manual trade (cf I Corinthians 1: 26–28, what was his attitude towards those who despised such workers? What would be his estimate of those today who look down on or (worse) patronize the "working classes"? Illustrate this tendency among a certain class of Church workers; why is it most harmful?

Christianity recognizes that poverty may have a dignity (cf. St Luke 6: 20–21), but (v. 12) there is no dignity in the poverty that comes from laziness. Illustrate the difference Why does St. Paul appeal to the estimate of "them that are without"? How far is their judgment important?

Compare Moffatt's version

51
4: 13–18 (1)

Even in the short time that the Thessalonians had been Christians, some deaths had occurred. Greeks, apart from philosophers and the members of certain religious societies, had no great hope in life after death Read this section. What consolation had Christianity brought?

With v 14 cf. Philippians 3: 10–11 (Study 22) for a fuller statement of the doctrine The margin gives an alternative rendering; copy the last clause with this alternative in it Does it seem clearer? The final "him" is "Christ," not "God"

v. 15 states, "The dead shall lose nothing of the final happiness"; how does this bear on v. 13? The picture in vv. 16–17 is complicated; first the dead rise to join the living, then dead and living alike are caught up. There are not two resurrections described. State vv. 15–17 in your own words, without trying to refine the language.

Note that everything in this section centers in Christ; the words "in Jesus" (v. 14) and "in Christ" (v. 16) explains how the resurrection can happen. Expand the doctrine in your own terms. "The dead in Christ rise to meet Christ, to be with Christ."

Why is there no mention here of the resurrection of the unrighteous? Would one who did not die in Christ rise naturally, or would a special miracle be necessary?

Compare Moffatt's version.

52–53

This little section belongs to what is known as "apocalyptic," the literature that pictures the end of the world. In the Dictionary read the article "Apocalyptic Literature," not spending much time on it. Read the article "Eschatology," more carefully with especial attention to sections 3 and 4, noting down the chief points. Read the article "Parousia," writing out all the New Testament references in full. Criticize the theories offered in section 3.

54
4·13–18 (2)

Observe that the Jews in New Testament days generally expected the end of the world very soon, and that Christians simply shared this Jewish conviction. Was it necessary that they should be taught differently? Inspiration corrects vital errors, but not "secondary" errors; God teaches men by direct inspiration only what they need know for their service of Him. Does this seem reasonable? How does Acts 1:6–7 support this doctrine? Did St Paul's inspiration give him any authority in matters of science? (But note that inspiration does not *teach* error; it only does not correct existing errors which do not matter practically)

Is it material that in v. 15 St. Paul expects the end to come in his life-time? In vv. 16–17 there are many details drawn from current Jewish belief, such as the "shout," "voice of the archangel," "trumpet," etc. (make a list). St Paul never thought of questioning these Jewish details. How far is our faith bound by them? Are they more than pictorial?

The specifically *Christian* teachings are that the resurrection is bound up with life in Christ, and that men in Christ lose nothing because of death Are there any other specifically Christian touches? How independent are these truths of the Jewish apocalyptic imagery?

State the argument of this Study in your own words.

55

Review of Chapter 4

(Cf. Study 8)

56

5: 1–11 (1)

Review 4: 16–17, and then read these verses. Although St Paul believed that the end would come soon, he made no claim to more precise knowledge. Cf St Mark 13: 32 In the Dictionary look up " Day of the Lord," and note down the chief facts (verifying the Biblical references). Cf. Philippians 1: 6, 10, 2: 16 In the last reference note the change of " Lord " into " Christ "; does this make any difference?

St. Paul goes on to apply "day" in the sense of " daylight "; state the meaning of v. 5 in your own terms What is the meaning of " sleep " in v. 6 (contrast 4: 13)? " Sober " is the opposite of " drunken "; what virtue is meant? Cf. Philippians 2: 15, Ephesians 5: 7–14 St. Paul is very fond of the figure of the Christian as a soldier (v. 8); cf. Romans 13: 12–14 and (especially) Ephesians 6: 10–18; he is thinking of Isaiah 59: 17. We know what earnestness in warfare means! Should we not develop the same zeal in the daily fight for righteousness? Illustrate. " The hope of salvation " is a helmet because confidence in victory is a splendid de-

I THESSALONIANS

fence; v 9 explains How does Philippians 3: 10–14 expand this?

What is the meaning of "sleep" in v 10? Note how v. 11 returns to 4. 18.

Compare Moffatt's version. In v. 4 he follows the "ancient authorities" noted in the margin of the Revised Version, "A" and "B" are the names of manuscripts What difference does this change make? Is it important?

57

5: 1–11 (2)

St Paul and the men of the Apostolic age generally lived in expectation of the near end of the world. This belief they held as Jews, but it received two Christian additions, (a) The universe will find its end in Christ, and (b) All men must give account to Christ. Expand these doctrines in your own terms. Compare them with the specifically Christian elements in the belief in the resurrection (Study 54). Can the Jewish belief in an immediate end of the world be separated from the Christian additions, the latter being held separately? Is it not a fact that Christianity always forbids a curious counting of the time of the end? In v 2 note St Paul's emphatic "perfectly" Compare St. Matthew 24·42–44, II St Peter 3. 10, Revelation 3:3, 16:15

As regards (b), above, does it make much practical difference whether Christ comes to judge us (at the end), or whether we go to Christ to be judged (at death)? Cannot we, then, apply these warnings of judgment practically by turning them into warnings to be ready for death? Illustrate, noting how "sudden destruction" (v. 3) and "watchfulness" (v. 6) can be made to fit into this application.

As regards (a), above, experience has taught us to be careful in our speculations. Christ is the End towards whom the whole creation moves; this is the specifically Christian dogma. But His triumph may be manifested in a single act, a series of single acts, or a long process (perhaps already begun). State each of these alternatives in your own terms. Which do you prefer, and why? Does it matter practically now which of them is true?

58

5: 12–15

Read these verses This is one of the rather rare occasions when St Paul speaks of the relations between "clergy" and "laity"; they were *all* his spiritual children, and he usually addresses them without distinction. Indeed, the line between clergy and laity was much vaguer then than in later years, for every layman felt it his duty to take some active part in the work of the Church. What disadvantages has the sharper separation of the two classes brought? What advantages?

In v 12 the "labor" was chiefly among the sick and the poor; explain. The position of "are over you" is curious (why?), and some scholars prefer to translate "care for you" (especially in financial or other support). "Admonish" is a correct translation; what class of workers would have this duty? Why did this class become obsolete? Apply the directions of v. 13 concretely to a faithful clergyman or parish worker. Would not such "esteem" often bring "peace"? Illustrate.

In v. 14 "disorderly" is a poor translation; the word means "idlers." Cf 4: 9–12 and (especially) II Thessalonians 3: 6–15 (read carefully, noting down the points of agreement with 4: 9–12).

This whole section is permeated with the idea of Christian *responsibility*. State this in your own terms, applying it to modern conditions

Compare Moffatt's version.

59

5: 16–28

Read these verses. With vv. 16–17 compare Philippians 4: 4–7, noting down the points of agreement

The four verses 19–22 are a unit; compare Moffatt's version, which is much clearer. In the Apostolic age extraordinary outpourings of the Spirit were common, often inspiring men to declare God's will. Unfortunately, these utterances were easily imitated by impostors, and men had to be constantly on their guard to test the "revelations"; cf. I St. John 4: 1–6, and explain its application. Just so today intense religious enthusiasm may be a cloak for all sorts of evil, although true religious enthusiasm is a precious gift. Expand and illustrate

v 23 is the only place in the Bible where "spirit," "soul" and "body" are found together. But they do not represent three essential parts of every human being, "spirit," when contrasted with "soul" is something that only believers possess, a "portion" of the Holy Spirit given them after conversion "May God preserve what is divine in you, together with your human personality" is the meaning. Expand this in your own terms.

Compare the closing benediction with Philippians 4:7, 19–20 Look up "kiss" (v. 26) in the Dictionary.

In v. 27 the earnestness of St. Paul's tone shows that he is not wholly satisfied, despite all his praise What indications of dissatisfaction are there in the Epistle?

Compare Moffatt's version.

60

Review of Chapter 5

(Cf Study 8)

61–62

Review of Studies 36–60

(Cf Study 31)

I THESSALONIANS

63

Review of the Epistle
(Cf Study 8)

64

Reread the Epistle, copying out all the important references to Christ. Arrange them so as to form a systematic series of statements. Compare the result with your work in Study 34. Philippians was written some twelve years later than I Thessalonians, to a much more mature church, are there any signs of this in the expressions used? (e g , in Philippians " Christ " is used 37 times, in I Thessalonians only 10 times). But is there any real difference in doctrine?

65

Review Philippians rapidly Write a brief description of St Paul's character as it appears in Philippians and I Thessalonians (do not forget his power of affection, his dignity, his sensitiveness). Do the twelve years that elapsed between the Epistles show any change in his character? Note particularly that the zeal of the later Epistle is as keen as in the former, remembering that St. Paul had worked for many years before he wrote I Thessalonians. Is such undiminished ardor common? What feature of St. Paul's character does it display?

Review Study 35 Amplify your results there from your study of I Thessalonians

FOR FURTHER STUDY

In the New Century series the volume on *Thessalonians* is by W. F. Adeney, and in the *Expositor's Bible* the corresponding volume is by James Denney. There are no important special studies of this Epistle that can be recommended otherwise for this course.

SECTION III

I CORINTHIANS 1–4

66–67

Note carefully the following facts:— I Corinthians was written from Ephesus, during St. Paul's Third Missionary Journey. It was written to a church that was some three years old, which had begun to develop independent difficulties. The Corinthians had written to St. Paul, asking his advice about some of the difficulties, and his reply is I Corinthians.

Copy these points in writing

Now read the Epistle through as a continuous whole, arranging your time so that this can be done without interruption.

68

Review Study 38

Read Acts 18:18–20:1, following St Paul's movements with the atlas. The Third Missionary Journey begins at 18:23, and I Corinthians was written in the period indicated in 19·10 In the Dictionary read the article "Ephesus," "Apollos," "Aquila and Priscilla," and note down the chief facts about each

Sum up in writing the events from St Paul's departure from Corinth until his departure from Ephesus.

69–70

Review Study 68. In the Dictionary read paragraphs 1, 2, 3, 10 of "Corinthians, First Epistle to the," noting down the chief points and looking up all the Biblical references. Read chapters 1–4 of the Epistle, making an outline as you read. Compare this outline with paragraphs 2 and 3 of the article in the Dictionary.

71

1 : 1–9

Read vv. 1–3. Compare them with Philippians 1 : 1–2 and I Thessalonians 1 : 1; the fuller form here corresponds to the fact that the Epistle is much more formal and elaborate The reason for the words " with all them," etc., in v. 2 is obscure, but they may be a warning against a spirit of independence, the Corinthians' great fault. Cf. 14 : 36, and explain how the words can be thus interpreted. Compare Moffatt's version. His conception of v 2 is different; does it seem more probable?

Look up " Sosthenes " in the Dictionary

The Corinthians laid great stress on " culture," priding themselves on their philosophical interpretation of Christianity Read vv 4–9 in this light, and compare Moffatt's version. " Utterance " in v. 5 is the power of expressing intellectual truths; show how such a power may be a most advantageous gift. How can it be abused? Why does St. Paul give thanks for his readers' "knowledge"? Note that Christianity is not at all meant for the simple and ignorant alone; illustrate.

Moffatt's rendition of v. 7 is very exact; all present gifts are but temporary The Corinthians do not possess *all* gifts, but they have so much of their own kind that the lack of the others is not felt Note the climax in v. 9.

Compare vv. 4–9 with I Thessalonians 1:2–7. What virtues are praised in the latter thanksgiving? Are they more or less worth having than those of Corinthian culture? The Church today has both "aristocratic" parishes and "enthusiastic" missions; state the virtues and the defects of each

72

1:10–17 (1)

The weakness of intellectualism is its tendency to divide men into parties; illustrate Read vv. 10–17 in this light.

Parties are inevitable, in some degree, wherever men work together. This is not wholly harmful, and, indeed, perhaps the best work may be done in the cooperation of groups of men of different sorts Illustrate. St. Peter ("Cephas") and St. Paul looked at many things differently, and on one occasion even came to a sharp quarrel (Galatians 2:11). But Galatians 2:9–10 expresses their normal relations; neither of them claimed a monopoly of Christianity. Their followers, however, accentuated their differences, as "small" men are apt to; illustrate.

From the Dictionary, pp. 156–7, paragraph 3, note down the characteristics of the different parties. Yet there was no reason why these different points of view might not work together in harmony. St. Paul does not exhort the three other parties to become "of Paul"; why not? Illustrate his principle from modern church life, noting how narrow zealots exaggerate points of division. (Yet there is a limit even to "inclusiveness.")

How many times is "Christ" used in vv. 1–10? How does this prepare for the exhortation to unity? How should the same principle apply today?

Compare Moffatt's version.

73

1 : 10–17 (2)

In Acts 10:48 who performs the actual ceremony of baptism? Apostles could no more give their time to detailed baptismal ceremonies than can bishops today; St. Paul observes sarcastically that this was lucky for him! Why? Does this indicate any low view of baptism on his part?

"In" (really, "into") "the name of N" is a formula that originated in ancient bookkeeping; it denoted the entry of an account on a page headed with

N's name. The items so entered were debited to his account as having become his property. Just so in baptism we are " registered " as the property of Christ. Explain this figure in your own terms.

Copy Romans 6:3, Galatians 3:27, and underline " baptized into Christ " This means " by baptism we become in Christ." Review Study 23 and explain the meaning of this phrase. How does it differ in sense from " baptized into the name of Christ "?

Explain the last clause of v. 13.

Write a little essay on the themes developed in vv. 10–13 as one basis for the reunion of Christendom today.

Compare Moffatt's version

74

1 : 17–25

Read these verses. In vv. 4–7 the intellectual attainments of the Corinthians were praised; here the dangerous side of these gifts is shown. But before attempting to evaluate these verses read 2:6–16 rapidly; it is enough to note that St. Paul asserts that Christianity has depths which tax the profoundest intellect. His point, consequently, is not a depreciation of the intellect He states emphatically, however, that man's intellect when unaided by God has gone wide astray; hence mere intellectual achievements are nothing to boast about. Expand this and illustrate it. How does it rebuke the Corinthians?

In shame crucifixion in the ancient world corresponded to hanging today; what is the paradox in "We are saved because a man was hanged"? Read Deuteronomy 21:23 and explain v. 23. How could Christian preaching be described as "foolish" (v. 21)? God chose this method to save the world, a method that man's "wisdom" would never dream of; why not? Explain v. 20. Explain v. 25, noting the irony there (is God ever "foolish" or "weak")?

Review Study 22; how does it bear on the present passage?

Compare Moffatt's version.

State the argument of vv. 17–25 in your own words.

75

1:26–31

Read these verses. Review Study 18, and compare it with this section (especially v. 29). What special application of "glorying in the flesh" is found here? How does a "foolish thing" put to shame them that are wise (v 27)? But note carefully that "foolishness" in itself is not commended; men sometimes glory in the flesh by boasting of being uneducated. Illustrate The "foolishness" is only what appears foolish when God's plan is not known.

The chief point is in v. 30. Whatever lack there may be in our endowments or opportunities can be made up (and more than made up) by what we find in Christ. By using the gifts found in Him, even the weak and simple can surpass the "wise" and "strong" Explain and illustrate. Show how this truth can give encouragement and joy to the most commonplace life. It is appropriate to sum up one aspect of the teaching here under the title "Christian democracy"; explain why

In v 26 is found the conception of God's "call"; cf. Philippians 3.14, I Thessalonians 2:12, 4:7, 5:24. This is closely connected with the doctrine of election, review Study 42 briefly. But too much time should not be spent on this theme, for the present, it is enough to realize that all our efforts would not bring us to God, if He did not lead the way.

Compare this section with St. Matthew 11:25–26, and note down the points of resemblance.

Compare Moffatt's version.

76

Review of Chapter 1

(Cf Study 8)

77

2:1–5

Read these verses. Note that they describe a special resolution formed by St Paul when he came to Corinth.

54 THE TEACHINGS OF ST. PAUL

Read Acts 17: 16–34, noting especially the learned, philosophical style of St. Paul's speech before the cultured Athenians. But did he make many converts (vv. 32–34)? Nothing is heard of a church in Athens in the New Testament. This was the only city where St Paul really failed, although he had done his utmost in "persuasive words of wisdom." From Athens, smarting with the sense of failure, he came direct to Corinth; how does this explain the resolution of v. 2? Did his change of method lead to better success? (Would it have led to better success in Athens?)

v. 5 is the kernel of the Epistle thus far; the heart of Christianity is its moral appeal. Men and women find many things in the expression of our religion that attract, intellectual stimulus (scholarly preaching, able books, etc), aesthetic gratification (music, ordered ritual, etc.), emotional delight (in some hymns, etc). Can you name other " subordinate " attractions? All these things are good and right, but they are not primary In the center of our religion is Christ, who cared so passionately for the things of God and so little for the things of the world, that He went unhesitatingly to the Cross.

What, then, is the final test of the sincerity of any person's Christianity (answer rather at length)? How would St. Paul's drastic reduction of our religion to its fundamentals be a test for modern parishes to pass?

Compare Moffatt's version The variation in v. 1 is unimportant.

I CORINTHIANS 1–4

78

2:6–16 (1)

These verses were glanced at in Study 74; review this Study briefly, and then read these verses. In the Dictionary read the article " Mystery," noting down the chief points, especially as they bear on the present section Write brief explanations of vv 7, 9, and 14.

In vv. 6 and 8 " the rulers of this world " appear. St. Paul refers to the Jewish belief in the partial control of this world by evil spirits. Copy these two verses, and add to them Ephesians 2:2, 6:12, St. John 12:31. What facts of experience could lead to belief in the " rule " of this world by powers of evil? Would they be conceived of as intensely intellectual beings, at least in the higher orders? Are they, therefore, fit examples of the extreme of unsanctified " wisdom "?

These "rulers" of course did not crucify Christ themselves (v. 8), but they tempted men to this act; has St. Paul's language any real inexactness? Did this act accord with their nature? But in persuading their victims to crucify Christ, they wrought their own overthrow; explain. So extreme ability and efficiency may lead to acts of the most extreme stupidity; illustrate from the history of the Great War.

State this doctrine of the " rulers " and their " wisdom " in your own words How does it help St Paul's rebuke of the Corinthians for their intellectual pride?

79
2:6–16 (2)

Review Study 78. Read vv. 10-16, which seem more difficult than they really are. Begin with v 11; does any human being really understand another? We all try to explain ourselves in words, but we often fail in conveying what is in our minds. Illustrate. If we are to be perfectly understood, we should have the power of "extending" our thoughts into the minds of others. But God has this power through the Spirit, which can inspire men with the thoughts of God. Explain.

The best understanding comes through sympathy, "feeling with" a person; the more like we are to a person, the better we can understand him. Illustrate. The work of the Spirit is to make men more like God, so giving them "sympathy" with God; no one can understand goodness except those who possess goodness. Illustrate. Now explain v. 12, noting that "the spirit of the world" is a mere pictorial phrase. Explain v. 13 (the margin is probably right).

In v. 15, "judgeth all things" of course means only "according to their spiritual value." St Paul's judgments on (say) geology would have had little value. But he was able to judge the spiritual utility of any doctrine, because of his "sympathy" with the guiding Spirit. Illustrate. So, e. g, we may be called to judge the value of some religious system. We may not be able to tell how much truth there is in its his-

I CORINTHIANS 1-4

torical or philosophical claims; these are matters for specialists. But we should be able to tell whether or not these claims will help to the appreciation of the essentials of Christianity. Illustrate.

The last clause of this verse is very incisive. Men call us "superstitious," "bigoted," "ignorant." If such judgments come from unspiritual persons, have they any importance? Would truly spiritual persons use such terms?

v 16 is in part a quotation of Isaiah 40:13; verify the reference. Note how the final clause is a cry of triumph; the ideal is one we should approximate more and more as life goes on.

State the argument of vv 6–16 in your own terms.

Compare Moffatt's version.

80

Review of Chapter 2

(Cf Study 8)

81

3:1–9

Read these verses. Compare vv. 1–3 with 1:4–9. The two passages are not contradictory, for a man of high attainments (1:4–9) may be a "babe" in understanding a moral question (3:1–3). Explain and illustrate Note the rebuke in v 2; "carnal" here means simply "un-Christian." The moral in v. 3 is very penetrating; persons who give way to jealousy and strife cannot hope to have any understanding of Christianity. And little respect need be paid to the opinions of such people. Illustrate. It is no excuse to say "we are only human"; if our religion has any meaning, we ought to be more than "only human" ("not carnal").

Review Study 72. It is good to be loyal to leaders But when this loyalty makes us overlook the good in those who are loyal to other leaders, then we are behaving like "mere men." Illustrate.

v. 5 states the ideal of our relation to religious leaders. We may owe them the greatest respect, devotion and affection; cf 4: 14–16. But no man is great enough to display *all* the attributes of Christ; we are "Christians," not "Paulians" or "Apollosians" Illustrate with some notorious violations of this principle. What should be our correct attitude?

vv. 6–7 give a classic statement of true leadership; not even the greatest can claim to be "anything" in comparison with God. Illustrate. Note St. Paul's generous warm heartedness towards Apollos. vv. 8–9 assert that no really great leader ever wants to be thought the *rival* of another great leader in a common work There is plenty of room for as many as possible in tilling God's field, in erecting God's building,—and each is finally responsible only to God.

State the argument in this section in your own words.

Compare Moffatt's version. Can you improve on "able" in v. 2?

82

3: 10-17

Read these verses. vv. 4–9 describe the relations between worthy leaders; this section treats of leaders who may not be so worthy. "Another" in v 10 is quite general; all sorts of persons in Corinth were endeavoring to pose as guides to the faith

There are many ways of expressing Christianity. And they all have some value, if they are built on the One Foundation. But the values differ very greatly; it is perfectly untrue that "one faith is as good as another" (v. 12). Illustrate Yet even the best need not be strictly uniform; a building of "gold" may be as worthy as one of "precious stones" Illustrate.

For "the day" in v 13 cf. Study 56. At the Judgment, the value of all expressions of Christianity shall be tested, the foolish as well as the wise, the saintly as well as the mediocre. How would the intellectual ideals of the Corinthians stand this test?

The picture in vv 14–15 is worth special attention The man in v. 15 is "saved,"— but all he can bring to Christ is his own poor soul Would one be proud of such a gift? Is not the end of our religion something more than personal salvation? State the better ideal; is it remembered frequently enough?

Note St. Paul's optimism about the salvation of even foolish Christians, provided they build on the right Foundation Is it unduly liberal?

One may build wisely, one may build foolishly,—

but one may destroy instead of building (vv. 16–17). Give illustrations of each of these acts. In v. 17 " destroy " is not to be pressed too rigorously; St. Paul is not interested in the future fate of the wicked, which he leaves vague (is not this the wisest plan?) In the last clause of v. 17 the margin gives the correct translation; cf. Ephesians 2: 19–22. Note the tremendous responsibility of our attitude towards the Church.

Compare Moffatt's version

83

3 : 18–23

Review Studies 74 and 77; then read these verses. A man becomes a " fool " (v 18) by putting off all intellectual pride, reducing his faith to its *moral* elements, and testing it by the Cross of Christ   Explain (be very careful to use the Cross as shaming the world, not here as the means of Atonement).   St. Paul concludes his argument with an appeal to prophecy; why does this make an excellent conclusion?   Cf. Job 5 : 13 and Psalm 94 : 11.

At the close, where a formal recapitulation might be expected, St Paul flashes out into a new line of thought   If I say, " I am of Paul," this is not only unjust to my relation to Christ   It is unjust to my own self. God's purpose is the salvation of men, and the leaders of Christianity have significance only as they assist in this process.   The clergy exist only for the benefit of the laity. Illustrate. Consequently, devotion to any man as a party leader is inconsistent with a layman's dignity Explain and illustrate.

Not only " Paul, Apollos, Cephas " are merely to serve our salvation, but everything created is to serve this purpose. Show how this idea is expressed also in Romans 8: 35–39. But note that the present passage is more positive; in Romans nothing can harm us, in the present passage all things exist for our service. Illustrate. Note the supreme climax in v. 23.

It is not well to spend much time in polemic, but it is impossible to overlook St. Paul's attitude towards St. Peter (" Cephas "). He respects him greatly. But how does he treat those who hold up devotion to St. Peter as of the essence of Christianity?

Compare Moffatt's version

84

Review of Chapter 3
(Cf Study 8)

85

Review of Chapters 1–3
(Cf Study 8)

86

The central theme of chapters 1–3 is unity in the Church. State St. Paul's principles in your own terms, and apply them to the problems of the present time. Does he expect uniformity? What is his attitude towards differences caused by merely intellectualistic theology? Towards differences created by the personality of party leaders? What should be the mutual attitude of those who think differently on non-essentials?

Yet does St Paul teach a vague indifferentism, which includes everybody, regardless of their character (3: 16–17, Philippians 3: 18–19)? And does he teach that allowable variations are all equally good?

(Note that the question of the Apostolic ministry is not raised; this was scarcely a problem in his day.)

Is his programme sufficient for the coordination of the parties within our own Church today? How far does it help towards Christian reunion in general?

87

4: 1–5

In chapter 4 St Paul pauses to answer certain attacks that have been made on him personally. II Corinthians 10: 10 gives a good idea of their nature; the Corinthians were inclined to patronize him, "a worthy man, but not educated!" Read chapter 4 through rapidly, and review the first five verses more carefully.

v. 1 is an expression of humility, not of pride; "we are *only* ministers, *only* stewards." What misconception of this verse is very common? How does this

I CORINTHIANS 1–4

verse sum up chapters 1–3? "The mysteries of God" are "the revelations of the Gospel"; cf 2:7.

v. 2 makes the transition to St Paul's self-defence "Even if we are only stewards, no one should accuse us of infidelity to our trust." How was the Corinthians' patronage of St. Paul an accusation of infidelity?

But in v. 3 he breaks off impatiently; "why should I trouble to defend myself?" Is not this the best attitude under much of the criticism one meets? But the precaution in v. 4 is necessary; we often abuse the truth by claiming clear consciences. Illustrate.

With v. 5 cf. St. Matthew 7:1–5. Yet it often becomes necessary to judge others! Only, we must first be sure that the necessity exists, and then make sure that our conscience is clean. What Our Lord (and, following Him, St. Paul) condemns is the habit of petty, shallow criticism. Illustrate. What is the Christian ideal of our attitude towards our neighbor's weaknesses?

Contrast St Paul's self-defence here with the much sharper terms of I Thessalonians 2:3–12. At Thessalonica he was charged with serious offences, in Corinth only with lack of ability. But the pettiness of this charge must have been exasperating, does it show in the tone?

Compare Moffatt's version.

88

4:6–13 (1)

Read these verses. v. 6 is very difficult. The general sense of "these things" is to be gathered from 3: 5–9; "I have spoken only of myself and of Apollos, but the same rule applies to the others as well" But the next clause we do not understand. Either there is some local allusion, or the text is corrupt; do not spend any time on this clause.

v. 7 is one of St. Paul's most perfect sayings. Explain and illustrate it. Even in purely earthly matters it is (at the best) stupid to boast of inherited privileges. In religion, such boasting may warp the whole spiritual nature Illustrate. Why do moralists generally count pride as the greatest of sins?

In v 8 St Paul passes to sharp sarcasm. "What beautiful progress you think you have made!" The "reign" is the serenity of heaven; the Corinthians behave as if they had become perfect Explain more fully. Then the sarcasm grows still sharper, "If you *were* in heaven, we poor Apostles might be there also, — and we need a little heavenly repose!" As a matter of fact, the Apostles' condition was the reverse of heaven (v. 9), they were suffering the greatest privations and humiliations These could be endured, but the patronizing ingratitude of the Corinthians was more than St Paul felt called on to bear. Explain. "Last," here, means "lowest"; condemned criminals were exposed to public derision. ("Angels" need not

I CORINTHIANS 1-4

be taken very seriously) Does " humility " mean readiness to accept *every* humiliation, regardless of its source or motive? When is it perfectly proper to protest?

Paraphrase vv. 6-9 in your own words; this difficult passage should receive special attention.

89

4:6-13 (2)

Review Study 88.

The sarcasm is continued in v. 10. Nothing is easier for an idler than to criticize workers, and few things are more contemptible. Illustrate. But in v. 11 the sarcasm is dropped. Read II Corinthians 11 as the best commentary on vv. 11-13 Explain how this chapter illustrates becoming " a fool for Christ's sake "; would " wisdom " point out such hardships as the natural fate of a great leader? How do St. Paul's words convict the Corinthians of ingratitude?

In the middle of v. 12 the appeal suddenly strikes a new note, the recompense of good for evil. But the final climax at the end reverts simply to the picture of sufferings; is this literary or conversational style? What is the meaning of the last half of v. 13?

Again note that St Paul does not protest at having to suffer. But he insists that those for whom he suffers shall not ignore his hardships.

Sum up the argument in vv 6-13
Compare Moffatt's version.

90

4: 14–21

Read these verses. Note St. Paul's calm after the outburst in vv. 6–13, although the tone hardens again in vv. 18–21.

v. 14 softens the reproof; explain it Note the perfection of the appeal in v. 15; cf. Galatians 4: 19. Why does v. 16 follow from v. 15? Cf Philippians 3: 17. St Paul refers to 3: 5–9 and 4: 9–13; "imitate my eagerness to work with others, and my readiness to accept sufferings." With v. 17 cf. Philippians 2: 19 and I Thessalonians 3: 2, 6. Note St. Timothy's "greatness in service." But the praise of St. Timothy helps us also to appreciate St. Paul; only a great and warm hearted man could acquire so devoted a minister. Illustrate. Compare the last clause of this verse with the last clause of 1: 2, and compare the note in Study 71. This warning against individualism (explain) effects the transition to the more severe tone of vv. 18–21.

Note v. 18's picture of the boldness of little men in the temporary absence of a great leader. Illustrate. In vv. 19–20 explain the antithesis between "word" and "power." The final threat in v. 21 is in no way inconsistent with intense affection; love that is not mere sentimentality does not shrink from necessary sternness. Illustrate.

Compare Moffatt's version.

I CORINTHIANS 1-4

91

Review of Chapter 4

(Cf. Study 8)

92

Chapter 4 is one of the most valuable for the study of St. Paul's character. It shows his humility together with his dignity, his readiness to suffer together with his unwillingness to suffer from " fools," his affection together with his severity. Collect the passages that show these aspects, and write a sketch of his character as indicated by them

93-94

Review of Studies 56-94

(Cf Studies 31-32)

95

Review of Chapters 1-4

(Cf. Study 8)

For Further Study

In addition to the New Century volume (by J. Massie) and the *Expositor's Bible* volume (by Marcus Dods) there is an excellent commentary by H. L. Goudge in the Westminster series (Gorham). The conclusions adopted in the present Studies often diverge considerably from those of these commentaries, so much so as to give the student a most interesting exercise in comparison.

The recommendations here apply also to the remaining sections of this course.

SECTION IV

I CORINTHIANS 5–7

96

Review Studies 69–70. Read chapters 5–7, and paragraphs 4–6 on p. 157 of the Dictionary. Extend your outline to cover chapters 5–7.

97

5: 1–5

Read these verses. This congregation, who prided themselves so on their attainments, were indifferent to a disgusting piece of immorality among them, where real Christianity would have thought first of righteousness. Illustrate.

The earliest churches were small, compact organizations, sharply marked off from the world, and the relations between the members were very close. Discipline, consequently, could be made the task of the entire community. Read Hebrews 12· 14–16, Galatians 6: 1–2, Colossians 3: 16, St. Matthew 18: 15–17, and describe the conditions under which such directions were practicable. In later days, the huge growth of the Church made such corporate action impossible, and disciplinary authority was necessarily left to the clergy alone. Explain. Does this change relieve laypeople from all responsibility for corporate discipline? Illustrate how lay action may become a duty.

In v. 4 note how careful St. Paul is to preserve customary forms, although he is acting on his sole authority. He assumes that he has summoned a "parish meeting," and that they have agreed on the action to take. Why can he assume this? Would he have thought it possible his converts would excuse so flagrant a sin, when called officially to their attention? Note the conception of the Church as a moral democracy, whose judgment is to be trusted What doctrine of personal responsibility is presupposed?

In v. 5 there is no doubt that St Paul threatens miraculous physical punishment on the guilty man. The power that could heal sickness could inflict sickness; of Acts 5: 1–11, 13: 9–12. But the purpose here is disciplinary, not punitive; explain the difference.

Compare Moffatt's version (the period at the end of v. 3 is a misprint for a comma.)

98

5:6–8

Read these verses. In the Dictionary read the article "Leaven," and note down the principal points. What is the meaning of "unleavened" in v. 7? The story of the institution of the Passover is of course familiar, but the memory may be refreshed by reading

I CORINTHIANS 5–7

Exodus 12: 1–13: 7. How did the mention of "leaven" lead St. Paul to speak of the Passover?

The Passover was a feast of deliverance, deliverance from the judgment on the Egyptians and from Egypt. What Christian deliverance has St. Paul in mind when he speaks of "our Passover"? Note that the Christian "feast" (v. 8) is lifelong. The "old leaven" is the "evil of unconverted days"; the addition of "of malice and wickedness" is only for emphasis and adds nothing to the sense.

Rewrite these verses, replacing the figurative expressions ("leaven," "lump," "unleavened," "passover") with the realities they are intended to represent. How does the exhortation bear on vv. 1–5?

Compare Moffatt's version.

99

5: 9–13

Read these verses. The Epistle referred to in v. 9 is lost, but some scholars think a fragment of it has found its way into II Corinthians as 6: 14–7: 1. What resemblance has this section to the present paragraph? Note that it has no relation to the context in II Corinthians.

Read Moffatt's version of II Corinthians 6: 14–7: 1. Ordinary business and social relations are not prohibited, only such close ties as can be described as constituting a "yoking together" Illustrate how such ties (apart from marriage) could exist. And in St.

Paul's day "unbelievers" naturally meant persons of low moral standards. State the principle involved, and explain how far it applies to conditions of the present day. Note especially the responsibility due to our privileges.

In I Corinthians (the present passage) a different aspect of the problem is treated. The unholiness of a degenerate believer is far worse than that of a frank worldling; explain and illustrate. How must St. Paul's directions be modified through the larger size of modern churches? How far can they be maintained? Illustrate.

vv. 12–13 are important. We are not responsible for the moral standards of the world at large, but we are distinctly responsible for the moral standards of our own religion. Explain and illustrate. In v. 11 note the special mention of "covetous" and "extortioner." Are we stern enough in our condemnation of riches unjustly obtained?

The last sentence of v. 13 returns to vv. 1–5. St. Paul can punish, but the withdrawal of relations must be the work of the Corinthians themselves.

Compare Moffatt's version.

100

Review of Chapter 5

(Cf Study 8)

I CORINTHIANS 5–7

101

6: 1–6 (1)

Read these verses. The general directions are clear enough; explain them Why are they impractical to-day? Modern law courts have faults enough, but are they professedly anti-Christian?

v 2 is taken from Jewish apocalyptic, but the thought is found elsewhere in the Bible; copy Daniel 7: 22, Wisdom 3.8, Revelation 20: 4. The picture is very realistic The Messiah descends to earth, and establishes His Kingdom among the men who are still alive, whether good or evil On the righteous devolves the privilege of bringing the world into obedience So they become the judges of the unrighteous, determining what room there is in them for repentance, what privileges may be accorded them, what punishment is due, etc. This is not the same as the doctrine of the Day of Judgment. Read Revelation 19: 11–20: 6, and compare it with 20: 7–15. At the final Day does any one join with God when He judges the world?

Two judgments, consequently, were expected by the Jews. After one a millennial Kingdom would be established on this earth, after the other the permanent life of heaven would begin. Only a partial resurrection would take place at the first judgment Read II Esdras 7: 26–34 very carefully, substituting " the Messiah " for " Jesus " in v 25 and for " Christ " in v. 29. Explain how this passage (written by a Jew, not a Christian) bears on the doctrine of a double judgment.

102

6:1-6 (2)

Review Study 101. The first clause of v. 3 is startling to modern readers, but a Jew of the time would see nothing strange in it "Angels" included not only the good spirits (as in Galatians 1:8) and the evil spirits (Study 78), but also spirits neither wholly good nor wholly evil (cf Ephesians 3:10, I St Peter 1:12) In the present case St Paul is probably (not certainly) thinking of evil angels, as in Study 78. When the world is put into order, these "rulers of the world" must be judged, or they would tempt men to wickedness again; of Revelation 20·7-8

State the presuppositions underlying vv 2-3a just as they were held, without attempting to interpret them for the present day Review Studies 51, 54, and 56 rapidly and Study 57 very carefully. What distinction was made in these Studies between the Jewish expectations and the specifically Christian beliefs?

103

6:1-3 (3)

Review Studies 101-102 carefully. In vv. 2-3 there is nothing that is *specifically* Christian; St. Paul has stated the current Jewish beliefs without modification. And yet his statements are not to be neglected on this

I CORINTHIANS 5–7

account The Jews looked forward not only to blessedness in heaven, but to a better future for this world also, and this expectation St Paul shared. Do not Christians generally share it? To be sure, St. Paul thought of a betterment brought in by a single act of God, and we think of a betterment through a progressive evolution guided by God But does this make any practical religious difference? Explain

St Paul thinks of Christians as judges who help establish the Kingdom, we think of Christians as agents who help the Kingdom develop, is there any essential religious difference? The heart of the doctrine is that the Church shall be the decisive force in the future betterment of the world. State this doctrine in modern terms of social progress. Some theologians have held that Christianity is concerned only with the final salvation of men's souls; is this an adequate definition? Where does it fall short?

5:12–13 is not in conflict with 6·2. As individuals we are not responsible for the condition of the world as we find it, but we have a very grave responsibility for its future. Give instances of means by which individuals can help in this task and privilege of the Church. What would the world be like, if Christianity should really triumph?

Something of the same imagery can be found in St. Matthew 19:28, but there it is really only pictorial and should not be stressed

104
6:1–6 (4)

Reread these verses. St Paul takes for granted that Christians should have a general understanding of the distinction between right and wrong in most matters. At least, they should know more than heathen magistrates! Even modern magistrates distinguish between "legal" and "illegal," rather than between "right" and "wrong." Explain the difference and illustrate. May not a legal victory sometimes mean a moral defeat? To some extent St. Paul's advice can be carried into effect today; a mutual spirit of conciliation, aided by wise advice, will obviate most lawsuits. Illustrate.

In this section the most important assumption is our duty to become "authorities" on moral questions. It is a duty we owe to others, as well as to our own souls: it is an imperative duty we owe to the world at large Explain. As means for acquiring this knowledge discuss the help to be gained from Scripture (especially from the teaching of Our Lord), from Church instruction (sermons, etc), religious experience (prayer and the sacraments), books on moral theology, treatises on scientific ethics, etc. How concretely is the need of such help felt by most laypeople?

One's own conscience is a safe guide only when it is enlightened by all the means within one's reach; explain. When should one *not* "follow one's conscience"?

Compare Moffatt's version.

105

6.7–11 (1)

Read these verses. v. 7 states a most important duty. One often hears litigants say, " I don't mind about the money, it's the principle of the thing." But the principle of self sacrifice is as important as any! Explain and illustrate. In v. 8 " ye yourselves " means especially the men condemned in v. 1. Note the bitter irony of this verse.

vv. 9–10 show us St Paul's method of teaching the elements of Christianity Converts were required to learn lists of sins that they must avoid, and the question, " Or know ye not? " is an ironical way of asking, " Have you forgotten your catechism? " The pedagogical method is stated explicitly in Galatians 5: 19–21, and a similar list appears in Romans 1: 29–32 Draw up a table of the sins named in these three lists, marking especially those that are found in two and those that occur in all three. Where was St. Paul's chief emphasis? Do there seem to be any important omissions?

106

6:7–11 (2)

Reread this section. v 11 has played an incredible part in theological controversies, and it deserves rather minute attention To begin with, it is clear that the three verbs " washed," " sanctified," " justified " denote events of the converts' *past*, events that took place for each at his entrance into Christianity.

"Washed" certainly describes baptism in its simplest aspect of cleansing from sin; copy Acts 22:16, Ephesians 5:26-27, I St Peter 3.21 (use Moffatt's version). These passages supplement each other admirably. In baptism our part is a prayer for a good conscience, which God answers by cleansing us from all our past sins. The rite consists of water and a "word" or formula. State the doctrine in your own words. Note that the cleansing occurs by God's act *in* baptism; the baptism is not a mere symbol of something that has occurred already.

"Sanctification" usually denotes a process that continues through our whole life (e g , I Thessalonians 4:3, 5:23), but here it denotes a single act (at the beginning) which gives the believer *possibilities* of holiness (e g, Hebrews 10·10, 13:12).

On justification review Studies 19-20 Why is something more than mere forgiveness implied in the present passage (vv 9-10)?

Review Study 73. But here the formula is "in" (*not* "into") "the name," and "in" means almost "by means of" Calling on the name of anyone was an appeal to his power (cf Acts 19:13) or a recognition of it (Philippians 2·10), and at baptism the name of Christ was always called on So here St Paul means "by the power of Christ, whom ye have acknowledged"

Paraphrase v. 11, explaining all the technical terms.

I CORINTHIANS 5–7

How is it related to vv. 7–10? Note St. Paul's appeal, "Be righteous, because ye have the power."

Compare Moffatt's version "Defeat" in v. 6 is very accurate. What is the meaning?

107

6: 12–20 (1)

The delicate questions in this section should be faced calmly and firmly. Review Study 49. Read these verses and compare Moffatt's version Note that in vv 12–13 he prints three sentences in quotation marks This is correct; these sentences were phrases used by the Corinthians ("catch-words").

"All things are lawful" is something that St. Paul himself taught in a certain sense: the Christian is bound by none of the old ritual laws Where in his writings is this doctrine most prominent? But the principle could very easily be abused, turning Christian liberty into license. Review Study 25. How do St Paul's replies in v 12 check such license?

The first clause of v 13 is a virtual quotation of Our Lord's words; read St Mark 7: 14–19 and show the relation. The Greeks very commonly drew a parallel between man's appetite and his passions, claiming that both were mere matters of the body, and hence morally indifferent How does this explain the last clause of v. 13? What (probably) were some of the Corinthians saying? Has this careless Greek doctrine any supporters today? Why is it so dangerous to adolescent boys and girls? A similar excuse is sometimes made for other sins of the body, such as gluttony, drunkenness, drug habits, some forms of laziness, etc. Illustrate.

108

6: 12–20 (2)

St. Paul's noble appeal in vv. 13–20 is so clear that it calls for very little explanation. vv. 13–14 make the obvious point that the resurrection body has no need of digestive organs, with the implication that the whole body is concerned in impurity.

In the Greek world unfortunate women were generally slaves, who had no legal control over themselves, and for whom consequently nothing could be done. So St. Paul could not argue from the injury done to womanhood.

v. 18 is not quite true; St. Paul has forgotten (e g.) drunkenness

Compare the argument here with that in Romans 6: 15–23. On the basis of both write an instruction for the use of the young.

109

Review of Chapter 6

(Cf. Study 8)

110

7: 1–7

St Paul now passes to the questions in the Corinthians' letter (v 1). Read the whole chapter rapidly and the first seven verses carefully.

The question is, "Is virginity a desirable state?" St. Paul replies, "Abstractly, yes,— but not in Corinth." How does v. 2 take up 6: 12–20? Married persons will understand vv. 3–4 without comment (cf. Exodus 21: 10), unmarried persons may pass over these verses. It should be observed, however, that St Paul is thinking only of normal persons in good health; exceptional problems should be solved with the aid of a physician

v. 5. Marriage in all its relations is holy and needs no apology. But husband and wife each remain separate personalities, with separate relations to God The practice St Paul mentions was common among the Jews; compare modern "retreats."

St. Paul's own vocation was so intense that the thought of marriage had never occurred to him (v. 7). But he recognized that even such a vocation did not exhaust all of God's gifts; married persons can acquire virtues which unmarried persons lack. Explain and illustrate. Note the absence of spiritual pride in this verse; have celibates always been so careful of others?

"By attempting to become angels, men sometimes become brutes." How does this saying apply here?

Explain it and illustrate. St. Paul never loses sight of the fact that men and women are human beings, with limits to their powers Do devotional writers always keep this in mind? Many devotional books were written for those called to monastic life; why are they often unprofitable to persons living in the world? Can you illustrate? But should the danger of exaggeration tempt into laziness? What is the proper mean for most of us? How can an exceptional vocation be tested?

Compare Moffatt's version

III

Before going on with the orderly sequence of this chapter, it is necessary to read vv. 29–31; they are presupposed in St. Paul's argument from v 8 on. Review Study 54

Now in vv. 29–31 the point is: —" The end of the world is so very near that it is scarcely worth while to change one's condition" Explain each clause in these three verses accordingly. Note especially the words " to the full " in v. 31. Why are they necessary?

Such teaching is known as " interim ethic," rules for conduct in the short interim before the end of the world. There are very few other instances of such ethic in the New Testament, and the present case is unique in its rigor. But, considering the expectations of the times, we are surprised in meeting so little of it. Define it in your own terms.

I CORINTHIANS 5–7

The advantage of this ethic lies in its extreme other-worldliness; explain and illustrate. Its disadvantage lies in its neglect of the future of this world; review Study 103 and explain. In particular, how would this ethic regard marriage (note that it would not think of providing citizens for coming generations)? What is the correct balance between an interim ethic and an ethic that looks only to this world?

Note that there is no interim ethic in Our Lord's teaching, although the Evangelists have given some of His sayings an interim coloring Compare St. Matthew 6: 19–21 with St Luke 12: 33–34. Which is the original form?

112

7:8–11

Review Study 111, then read these verses. In v. 9 "burn" means "suffer continual temptation." Temptation of course is not sin, but continued temptation is dangerous; illustrate. And this particular temptation points to marriage How does St Paul's doctrine avoid morbidity? What other impulses point towards marriage? How far can interim ethic be responsible for St. Paul's omitting them?

vv. 10–11 are a quotation from Our Lord's words; how is this quotation indicated? Read St Mark 10: 2–12 carefully, verifying the reference to Deuteronomy 24: 1–4. Note that in Israel divorce was a private matter; a man might dismiss his wife without judicial proceedings of any sort; Christ was teaching private morality, not public law. The hearts of many men today are quite as hard as those of the Israelites to whom God permitted divorce; how far need we trouble ourselves about the permission of divorce by civil legislatures? For followers of Christ, however, there can be no "divorce problem"; St. Paul cannot even discuss the matter, for Christ has spoken on this subject. Why is "not I, but the Lord" final?

Read St. Luke 16: 18, St Matthew 5: 31–32, 19: 3–9. What do these passages add to the accounts in St. Paul and St. Mark? Scholars are generally agreed that the "exceptional clause" in St. Matthew expresses the interpretation of Christ's words in the Palestinian church? Does this seem reasonable?

Compare Moffatt's version of all the passages cited above

113

7: 12–14 (1)

These three verses seem complicated because they deal with terms that are unfamiliar to us. Before studying them read Deuteronomy 7: 1–5 and Ezra chapters 9–10. Copy Ezra 9: 2. Does "holy" here mean "in a state of salvation" or simply "dedicated to God"? No Jew could marry a Gentile; does this have any bearing on the moral character of any particular Jew? I.e., "holy" here is a *ritual* term

Now read the verses of the present Study. To St. Paul the Christians were the "holy ones," who had replaced the Jews in this prerogative. Hence the problem of mixed marriages now arose for Christians. So explain the meaning of "sanctify" and "holy" in v. 14.

The general principle, then, is that the "holiness" of Christians cannot be injured by ordinary contact with the world; instead, it imparts something of its own quality to the world. Express this in moral terms, and illustrate it How does it express a duty? What are the limitations of this principle, as regards "sanctifying" things that are evil in themselves?

114

7: 12–14 (2)

With v. 12 compare v 25 and contrast v. 10. What does St Paul mean by "I, not the Lord"? He hesitates about speaking with full assurance; these are new questions, and he is not quite sure of his ground (v. 40). Not even inspiration will give us an answer to all conceivable moral questions Contrast this hesitancy with the boldness in 2: 15 (and the note on this verse in Study 79) In some instances, all we can do is to point out what seems to us to be best, while admitting that other courses may be equally right. State this principle in general terms, and illustrate it. Clergymen are often asked to give off hand judgments on the most complicated questions; is this fair? Is it right to argue that Christianity *must* have some final court of appeal for all problems?

In v. 10 the assumption is that the children of even

one Christian parent are "holy." Read St. Mark
10: 13–14; how does this explain St. Paul's assumption? Review Study 113; does the "holiness" here necessarily merit final salvation? Would it dispense with the necessity of baptism? (A believing wife might not be able to win her husband's consent to the baptism of the children) Has the verse any bearing at all on infant baptism? (A baptized child would not only be "holy," it would be "in the Lord," as in Colossians 3: 20, explain the difference.)

Do Our Lord's words in St. Mark contain any restriction as to the parentage of children? Is St. Paul as wide hearted? (But the Apostle deals only with the practical problem presented to him.)

Compare Moffatt's version; note his very careful choice of terms.

115

7: 15–16

Read verses 12, 13, 15, 16 as a whole, omitting v. 14; in vv 15–16 the unbelieving partner is not "content to dwell" with the believer. In this case the latter is not bound to contest divorce proceedings; hope of converting the unbeliever is too uncertain to justify the distress of a contest State this advice in your own terms. Roman Catholic theologians hold that in this case (under certain restrictions) the believer may marry again (the "Pauline prerogative"), but modern scholars generally (not always) incline to

I CORINTHIANS 5–7

the opposite opinion Review Our Lord's sayings in Study 112 and form your own opinion.

The last clause of v. 15 states the principle on which St. Paul's advice rests; no one is held to attempt the impossible, or even the highly improbable. God wishes His servants to enjoy peace. Copy St. Matthew 11:28–30, St. Mark 5:34, St Luke 7:50, St. John 14:27, 16:33. Review Study 26 rapidly. State in your own words the Christian ideal of peace How is it to be attained? How far can this right to peace be used in refusing to undertake an over-burdensome task? How can this right be abused (cf, e g, St Matthew 10:34)?

Compare Moffatt's version. But his rendition of v. 16 has few defenders, the Greek text contains nothing corresponding to the "not." How does he change the sense?

116

7:17–24 (1)

Review Study 111, then read these verses. How do vv. 17 and 24 state an interim ethic doctrine? The last clause of v. 21 is very obscure, but the sense seems to be likewise based on interim ethic, "nay, even if you can become free it is better to keep your present condition, the matter is not important enough to warrant a change." The drawback to this ethic here is its tendency to weaken legitimate ambition; its advantage is that it tends to peace State the arguments on both sides.

THE TEACHINGS OF ST. PAUL

But, after all, any Christian ethic must be to a great extent an interim ethic; earthly advantages at the best can be only temporary, and for the highest realities we look to the world to come. And most human beings never have it in their power to alter their worldly condition very materially, despite many notorious exceptions. Note, moreover, that St Paul does not endorse an idle indifference to worldly things; he insists on the dignity of even the lowliest avocation "A slave is Christ's freeman; no rank can be higher than this" Expand and illustrate.

The kernel of the section is in v. 23 Most men could be satisfied with their lot, were it not for the desire to excel others Restless striving for worldly advantage,— what is it but a slavery, a slavery to other men's opinions! Explain and illustrate What have we, bought with Christ's blood, to do with such a slavery? Contentment in a modest station may be the truest dignity and independence. Illustrate.

State the argument of vv. 17, 20–24, in your own words, without regard to the interim ethic basis.

Compare Moffatt's version. His interpretation of v. 21 is less probable than that adopted above, but it is quite possible.

117

7: 17–24 (2)

vv 18–19 present a special problem, which has already been glanced at in Study 21. Review this Study.

I CORINTHIANS 5-7

Copy v. 19, Galatians 5:6, 6:15 A general principle is stated with finality. v. 18 gives a general rule for applying this principle (to "become uncircumcised" probably means only to "live like a Gentile") Read Acts 16:1-3 St. Paul violated his own rule in this case in order to secure an assistant who could work acceptably among Jews; does this seem a sufficient reason for the violation? Note that there was no thought that circumcising St. Timothy made him any more acceptable to *God* Read Acts 21:17-26. In Gentile communities St Paul paid no attention to the Jewish Law, but in Jerusalem he was perfectly willing to conform to it. How does the present passage in I Corinthians show the falsity of the charge in Acts 21:21? Was there any real inconsistency in St Paul's conduct? Our modern churches have very different degrees of ceremonial; show how St. Paul's rules and practices can be applied by modern Churchmen under various circumstances.

Normally ceremonial is only the outward expression of varying devotional methods, of little objective importance. But it may be the outward expression of vital doctrine, and, in this case, it may become a field of legitimate controversy Read Galatians 2·11-16, 5:1-12 (without pausing too much over details). What created the difference in attitude? In particular, how do you reconcile Galatians 5:2 with Acts 16:3? It is a characteristic of small minds to insist on uniformity of conduct in minor details, without realizing that identical outward acts may represent very different principles, or that the same principle may lead to opposite outward acts under different circumstances. Explain and illustrate.

118

Review of 7: 1–24

(Cf. Study 8)

119

7: 25–40 (1)

It is clear that this section is a reply of St. Paul's to the Corinthians' question, " What shall we do about virgins? " What these " virgins " were is uncertain. There are two theories One is that fathers asked, " What shall we do about our unmarried daughters? " This theory is adopted in the Revised Version. The other theory assumes that a custom of the later Church existed already in Corinth, the so-called " spiritual marriage " custom, in which the parties lived together as brother and sister. This theory is adopted in Moffatt.

Read both versions through very carefully, and compare them closely in vv. 36–38. What are the arguments that can be used for or against each theory? Which seems to you to be more probable?

120

7 : 25–40 (2)

Review Study 111 carefully, and then read verses 25–31. In v. 26 the words "that is upon us" are rightly rendered by Moffatt as "imminent"; the distress had not yet come, but St Paul expected it at any time ("present" in the King James version is a mistake). Jewish eschatology almost invariably looked for a period of intense suffering before the end; read (rapidly) St. Mark 13 : 3–27 and Revelation chapters 7–8, and name some other passages teaching the same doctrine. How does St Mark 13 : 20 explain v. 29 of the present passage (note that both mean, "The end will come sooner than men expect")? How would this doctrine influence St. Paul's advice?

The passage otherwise needs little expectation. In v. 27 "bound" means "betrothed," not "married"; how do vv. 10–11 prove this? And "loosed from a wife" means simply "unmarried." In v. 28 the principle is, "It is not wrong to choose a lesser good, when a greater good is also possible." Generalize this principle and illustrate it, noting that the "lesser good" must be *good*

v. 25 is an interesting proof of the care with which Our Lord's words were preserved in the early Church St. Paul knows them all, and knows they contain nothing bearing on the question of "virgins" Are we always as careful to distinguish between what is actually revealed and what simply seems right to us? Illustrate the great dangers that can come through neglecting this distinction.

121
7:25-40 (3)

Read verses 32-35. Note the marginal variant (note 5); it is interesting, but the text is correct Observe Moffatt's rendition.

St Paul's meaning here is self evident; give illustrations of his statements. Note that he uses two main arguments, "you will have greater comfort" (v. 32, cf. v 28), and "you will be free to serve God" (v. 35). The first of these is partly based on interim ethic, explain. In part it is independent of this ethic, does not marriage involve grave responsibilities? But in the second argument there is no interim ethic; is not this rule universally true? It has certain obvious exceptions, such as that of a woman unable to support herself (name some others), but it needs very little qualification

This raises the question of "vocation," God's special call to individuals to lead lives of special voluntary consecration. Such opportunities are provided in every part of the Church; sisterhoods, monasteries, deaconesses, missionaries, special workers of all sorts Illustrate for both Catholicism and Protestantism. And many individuals dedicate themselves to such special service apart from any order or society. State rather fully what you consider to be the ad-

I CORINTHIANS 5–7

vantages and drawbacks of such a life, in the view of what St Paul says and in view of modern conditions. Need such a life be dedicated by any special vow? What are the advantages and disadvantages of a vow?

122
7: 25–40 (4)

Review Study 119 carefully. In addition to the two theories stated there a third may be mentioned. Among the poorest classes of the ancient world a little girl was frequently sold into slavery for a very small sum, and unmarried men with little money often resorted to such a purchase to have their homes cared for. As the girl grew older a problem would arise; note that in v. 36 "past the flower of her age" merely means "old enough to be married" Explain the passage on this basis Does it seem a practicable theory?

Note that most Corinthians would not have recognized there was any "problem"; a girl of this class had no legal rights Write a short essay on what Christianity did for the dignity of girlhood and womanhood.

vv. 39–40 are a separate note, dealing with widows There is a little sarcasm in the final verse, which Moffatt brings out ably.

123

Review of 7: 25–40

(Cf. Study 8)

124

Review of Chapter 7

(Cf. Study 8)

125

The importance of the interim ethic doctrine warrants a special review of this theme by itself. Define interim ethic, and illustrate it Such doctrine has led to great folly in some adventist bodies; can you illustrate? Scholars generally hold that an instance of such foolishness is rebuked in II Thessalonians 3: 6–12; read this passage and explain it. Note very carefully how St. Paul was protected against running into such an error. His directions might occasionally be imperfect; illustrate from I Corinthians 7. But they are never wrong headed; how is he careful to say that he is giving only his own opinion? And his directions always contain much absolute truth; vv. 32–35, e g., are free from interim limitations. Moreover, the certainty of death for us all gives to all our ethic a true interim coloring.

State all this more fully in your own words

Write a little essay showing how God's inspiration

can use a human misconception, purify it from harmful elements, and bend it to His service.

126–127

Review of Studies 96–125

(Cf. Studies 31–32)

128

Review of Chapters 5–7

(Cf. Study 8)

129

Chapters 5–7 are especially interesting for their picture of St. Paul as a teacher who gives detailed instructions to men regarding their conduct Write an essay bringing out this side of his character, noting the methods he uses (explaining, reasoning, pleading, exhorting, commanding, threatening, etc.), giving exact references to the passages cited.

SECTION V

I CORINTHIANS 8–11

130

Review Studies 69–70 and 96. Read chapters 8–11, and paragraph 7 (with the first section of paragraph 8) on pp. 157–158 of the Dictionary. Extend your outline to cover chapters 8–11.

131

8: 1–6

The Corinthians wrote, " What about food offered to idols "? In the Graeco-Roman world it was a common practice to dedicate food to a deity, usually by placing it before his statue, pronouncing a prayer and (often) sprinkling it with consecrated water. Such food was supposed to have some vague sort of supernatural power, which would benefit the eater. The rite was often very informal, and dealers sometimes dedicated their wares before offering them for sale (10:25). Sometimes the dedication was very elaborate, taking the form of a banquet, which might be held in a temple (v 10) Banquets of this kind were

I CORINTHIANS 8–11

not uncommon, and to refuse to share in them meant being cut off from many social and business privileges Describe the custom in your own words

Read verses 1–6, and compare Moffatt's version. The passages he puts in quotation marks are extracts from the Corinthians' letter; write them out as a continuous statement The Corinthians argued that they might eat such food and even join in such banquets, for " an idol is nothing, as we all know, and a ' nothing ' cannot defile us." Is this argument plausible? Is it convincing?

St Paul is irritated by the Corinthians' boast of " knowledge "; what criticisms did he make earlier in the Epistle? Note in v. 3 the curious turn, " You boast of knowing God; does God know *you?*" What does this mean?

In v. 5 St. Paul expresses no doubt that various " gods " and " lords " really exist. What does he mean? Where have we met this before? But in v. 6 he goes on to say that they have no importance; does this amount to a *practical* denial of their existence? Review Study 10; what does the present section add to the concept " Lord "? Review Study 13.

132

8:7–13 (1)

Read these verses The kernel is in v. 7 (copy it), in which St Paul makes a very important point: — An act may be harmless in itself, but it may become harmful to a man who believes there is sin in it. Read the fuller discussion of this theme in Romans 14, copying v. 14 Explain this verse, noting that it quotes the saying in St. Mark 7: 14–19. Copy Romans 14: 23. "Not of faith" means "not with a clear conscience"; explain this verse. Read Moffatt's version of Romans 14, without comparing it closely.

Problems of this sort often arise for those who have been brought up strictly in such matters as rigid Sunday observance, abstinence from dancing, etc. Laxer rules may be harmless (or even beneficial), but to tempt persons of a rigid upbringing into breaking the rules may lead them to think they are sinning,— in which case they *are* sinning. Explain and illustrate. State St. Paul's principle in your own words.

133

8: 7–13 (2)

Review Study 132. After stating the principle of v. 7, St. Paul goes on to ask (v 8), "Why make such a point of this? You argue as if there were virtue in the brazen eating of food of this sort!" A man who learns that he may do something he thought was sinful is prone to run to the opposite extreme; illustrate. Explain vv. 9–10 and illustrate them in modern life. v. 11 elevates the discussion to the higher plane of thoughtfulness for others. What passages in Romans 14 are similar? v. 12 raises the discussion to the very highest plane; illustrate again from Romans

14. Illustrate v. 13 from Romans 14, and explain how the rule may be applied in modern life

State the argument of this section in your own words.

Compare Moffatt's version

134
Review of Chapter 8
(Cf. Study 8)

135
Chapter 9

At first sight this chapter appears to be an irrelevant digression, but in reality it forms an essential link in the argument. In 8: 13 St. Paul laid down this rule, " It is often necessary to give up what is lawful, in order to help others " The immediate moral is, " You should be willing to leave idol food alone, in order to help those who are weak " Read this chapter very carefully, and make a list of the examples St. Paul uses in proving his point.

136
9: 1–2

St Paul's argument is, " An Apostle has special rights, but I have been satisfied to lay them aside." This reminds him that some have questioned his authority, which he proceeds to defend.

His third question is important. Read Acts 1:15–26. In vv. 21–22 (copy them) what conditions are named for choice to the office of Apostle? St. Paul had not technically fulfilled these conditions; explain how his enemies could use this fact. Read I Corinthians 15:1–11; how does this explain the question, "Have I not seen Jesus our Lord?" In this section (cf v. 7 with v 5) note that "Apostle" has a wider sense than the Twelve; the missionary work of the Church had grown so that additional Apostles had become necessary.

In the present section compare v. 2 with 15·10 "An Apostle's business is to found churches" How does St. Paul use this definition in his defense?

In the Dictionary read the article "Apostles," and note down the principal facts.

137

9:3–15 (1)

Review Studies 28 and 44, then read these verses. St. Paul's rule about refusing to take money had been perverted by his enemies, who said "He does not *dare* to ask for pay; he knows he has no right to an Apostle's prerogatives." Explain the meanness of such a charge, and its perversion of an heroic virtue into a cowardly vice. Is St Paul's tone of indignation too extreme? Compare I Thessalonians 2·5, noting that he had to face unscrupulous attacks from both directions. Are we not inclined to overidealize the righteousness of the rank and file of the Apostolic Church? Cannot a very pessimistic picture be drawn from the references in St. Paul's writings? Illustrate. But such a picture would be unfair. An Apostolic church was much like the average parish of today, good and bad, generous and envious mixed; but in spite of that the good was sufficient to enable it to conquer the world. Need we ever despair about the mixed conditions in the Church of today?

In v 4 the "right to eat" is of course the "right to demand support." Similarly in v. 5 the "right" is "sufficient support for a married man." The Apostles were normally married, celibacy among Jews was extremely rare. Compare St. Mark 1:30 and (quite possibly) I St. Peter 5:13 (margin). St. Barnabas (v. 6) shared St. Paul's rule, for reasons that are not known. These two Apostles had been close friends; in the Dictionary read the article "Barnabas" and note down the chief facts.

138

9:3-15 (2)

Review Study 137. With v 7 St. Paul generalizes his theme, and in v. 8 appeals to Biblical support; state these two verses in your own words. The use of the Old Testament in v 9 is curious St. Paul quotes Deuteronomy 25.4 (verify the reference), which he treats as a Rabbi might: — Oxen are not important enough to warrant a special command of

God, therefore there must be a higher meaning to the verse. Is this use of the Old Testament convincing to us moderns? Why not?

Exegesis is as much a science as medicine, and St. Paul simply used the scientific methods of his own day. Contrast Our Lord's method of using a similar argument in St. Matthew 6. 25–30, a splendid example of the difference between a saint and the King of Saints Explain. In the Dictionary read the article " Quotations " rapidly.

v. 14 probably quotes the saying in St. Matthew 10: 9–10.

State the argument in vv. 3–14 in your own words, and apply it to modern conditions.

Compare Moffatt's version

139

9: 16–18

Read these verses; they are difficult In v. 16 the " necessity " is God's call; when He speaks, it is no merit for men to obey. Explain. Men often display irritation and peevishness in following God's call (illustrate); how does this verse protest against such an attitude?

In v. 17 " stewardship " expresses lowliness, not loftiness, of rank; cf. 4: 1–2 and the notes in Study 87. Compare St. Luke 17: 7–10; how is this little parable related to St. Paul's words? The second clause of v. 17, then, means, " What I do under God's compulsion has no more merit than a slave's obedience." To win reward one must go beyond compulsion and do some voluntary act; in St Paul's case this took the form of refusing pay. Compare St Luke 6: 32–35, and explain how this passage illustrates St. Paul's words.

Compare Moffatt's version, which is not wholly satisfactory. Make a paraphrase of your own, which will present St. Paul's thought clearly. What should be one's attitude on assuming a trying duty?

140

9: 19–22

Review Study 133, then read these verses. After the elaborate exposition in vv. 1–18, St Paul begins to apply its results to the theme of chapter 8. "Free," in v. 19 is explained in vv. 20–22. As a member of Christ St. Paul was under no obligation to conform to the Law (v. 20), to behave like a Gentile (v. 21), or to act like those with tender consciences (v. 22); as regards such obligations he was "free." What, then, is the meaning of "bondage" in v. 19? Paraphrase this verse, and show how it bears on the question raised in chapter 8.

On v. 20 review Study 117. The best commentary on v. 21 is given in Romans 2: 14–15; show how this reference applies, and explain the verse. v. 22 is illustrated admirably by Acts 16: 1–3; explain Note that being "all things to all men" not infrequently involved St. Paul in the necessity of painful self-sacrifice; explain.

All conduct involves a continual conflict between two principles; the free development of the individual, and the welfare of the social group. State the Christian aspect of this problem in your own words, and indicate how the antithesis is to be reconciled. Did St. Paul carry his "bondage to all" to the point of sacrificing his personal dignity and reputation? What is the practical limit in this regard?

Compare Moffatt's version.

141

9: 23–27

Read these verses. So far St Paul has appealed only to the good in the Corinthians, but he now closes with a note of warning; "too much liberty may result in the loss of salvation." But with admirable tact he words the warning as if it concerned himself alone; why is this an excellent method? Review Study 22 and note the similar tone, although here the implied blame is more explicit.

The figure in v. 24 is perhaps inexact; why? But it may be made precise by supposing that we race not with other men but with our evil habits; explain it on this basis. v. 25 gathers up the whole argument since 8: 1 in two sentences, explain the figure, and show how it bears on the Corinthians' question in 8: 1. How can it be made to apply to the spiritual life in general? Note the reproach; can we not give as much zeal to the things of God as we give to mere sports?

Zeal alone is not enough, it must be directed and intelligent zeal (v. 26). This verse and the next are often (and rightly) used as mottoes for Lenten discipline, etc. But a severe Lenten discipline often leads nowhere; fasting, for instance, is completely useless unless it has a definite purpose Give an illustration of such unintelligent zeal. But St. Paul scarcely has fasting (etc) in mind, he is thinking of the discipline and struggle that comes in fulfilling the precepts of vv 19–22; explain But show how private disciplinary practices can help to a self-controlled character.

Compare Moffatt's version

142
Review of Chapter 9
(Cf. Study 8)

143
10: 1–13 (1)

St. Paul now returns explicitly to the question of 8·1. The Corinthians have written (or implied), " Our sacraments protect us from any harm, even when we join in an idolatrous banquet." St. Paul replies, " The Jews had sacraments, too, but they sinned none the less"; read vv 1–13 and explain the argument in a general way.

In Study 138 review what was said about St. Paul's use of the Old Testament. A still more interesting example is found in the present section.

Read Exodus 13: 21–22, 14: 19–30; in this narrative is the Cloud *over* the Israelites? What is the case in Psalm 105: 39, Wisdom 10: 17? Which tradition does St. Paul follow? Was it not natural to follow the later tradition? What is a cloud made of? Explain, then, how "in the cloud and in the sea" can be spoken of as a "baptism" (by immersion). St Paul uses a tradition that was common among the Rabbis; when the Israelites left Egypt they were in need of purification (why?), and so they were made to pass through cleansing water. Was this a natural thought? But note that it adds something to the narrative in the Old Testament.

Review Studies 23 and 73 What does "baptized into Christ" mean? St. Paul writes "baptized into Moses" on the analogy of "baptized into Christ"; why is it inexact (could anyone be baptized "into" Moses?)? Can it mean much more than, "they accepted Moses as their leader"?

In the Dictionary read the article "Baptism."

144

10: 1–13 (2)

v 3 requires careful study. Read Exodus 16, and note down the principal characteristics of the manna. Which of them could be shared by natural food?

I CORINTHIANS 8–11

Which of them were definitely miraculous? Where did the manna come from? Copy Psalm 78.23–25 (substituting "angels" for "mighty"); what is the conception of the manna here? How does it advance beyond the description in Exodus? Copy Psalm 105: 40; does this add anything? Copy Wisdom 16:20; does this add anything? (Do not be surprised by the conception of "angels' food." Compare St Luke 22: 28–30, Revelation 22:2; how do these passages explain the phrase? To us of course it is only figurative, but most Jews took it literally.)

What, then, was the common belief about the manna among the Jews of St Paul's day? Was this magnifying a great miracle of the past natural? Can you give examples of similar glorification of great historic acts? Is there any reason to suppose that St Paul did not share the belief in such stories?

In the Dictionary read the article "Manna"

145

10: 1–13 (3)

v. 4 seems bewildering, and needs special explanation Read Numbers 20:2–13 But the wilderness of Sinai is waterless almost everywhere, not only at Meribah; how did the Israelites obtain water elsewhere? The Rabbis taught that the rock of Meribah accompanied the wanderings, like the manna And many fantastic stories were told about this rock, for (of course) it must have been miraculous to the highest degree. In the Dictionary read the article "Rock" (first paragraph).

Now, just as the Jews believed that the manna was angels' food, so they believed that the water from this rock was angels' drink. Copy Revelation 22: 1, and from this show how St. Paul could say "the rock was Christ." The passage now should be fairly clear; explain it Note how naturally St. Paul speaks of Our Lord as active before the Incarnation.

Review Study 144, and write an extended paraphrase of vv. 3-4, stating in full the stories that St Paul presupposes (omit the word "spiritual").

146

10: 1-13 (4)

Review Study 145 What are the usual meanings of the word "spiritual"? Look up I Corinthians 15: 44; does the sense of "spiritual" here come under any of the definitions just written? A "spiritual body" is evidently a body such as angels have, and "heavenly body" gives the exact sense (cf. I Corinthians 15: 40) Now in the present section in vv. 3-4 for "spiritual" substitute "heavenly." Does it make good sense? Is it a satisfactory translation? Both the manna and the water were food for the body, with heavenly qualities. How does "spiritual food" in this sense differ from its modern meaning, as in the phrase "Bible reading is spiritual food"? Distinguish these two senses very carefully; it is most confusing to read the modern force back into St Paul But note that v. 5 shows that St Paul believed that the manna and the water strengthened the soul also; why?

Compare Moffatt's version of vv 1–4.

In vv. 1–2 St Paul presents a type of baptism, in vv. 3–4 he presents a type of the eucharist From the material in the present Study and in the last two state what can be gathered about his belief in the effects of Holy Communion. Note that he naturally believed the actual sacrament was more supernatural than its type.

147

10: 1–13 (5)

Review Studies 143–146

All Israelites, good and bad alike, were brought into contact with spiritual benefits in the gifts detailed in vv. 1–4. Now read v. 5–13 With v. 6 cf. Numbers 11·4–6, 31–34. With v 7 cf Exodus 32:1–6, 25–28; "play" means "indulge in drunken dancing, etc." With v 8 cf. Numbers 25:1–9; St Paul's "23000" is probably a slip of memory With v 9 cf Numbers 21:4–9 With v. 10 cf. Numbers 14.

Write briefly on St. Paul's intimate knowledge of the Old Testament

Compare v. 11 with 9:9–10 and the note in Study 138. The theory of this verse is that, at the end, all sacred history was gathered up to find its application;

any part of the Old Testament was meant to have a meaning for the Apostolic age. State this theory in your own words. It is even truer than St. Paul knew; in every age the moral problems of all the preceding ages are repeated. In many things we progress, but the questions of right and wrong do not vary much; explain. Write on the utility of the study of sacred history for help in answering moral questions.

148

10: 1–13 (6)

Review Study 147 and (more rapidly) Study 131. All of the references in vv. 6–10 are meant to refer concretely to the question of sharing in idolatrous banquets (8: 10, the more general question of food merely offered to idols is not in point here). For instance, such banquets were often licentious (v. 7), and they should be avoided without discontent (v 10). Rewrite vv. 6–10 and make the application explicit in each case. Then show how v. 11 applies, and that the moral of v. 12 is intensely applicable to the situation.

v. 13 shows that a real deprivation was involved when such banquets were avoided; note that St Paul is genuinely sympathetic. But duty is plain Put this in your own words

Compare Moffatt's version of vv. 5–13.

The general principle raised in vv. 1–13 is the danger of presumption, and of running needlessly into temptation. Give some modern examples of this tendency, such as using improper books, dangerous places of amusement, etc. What is the proper attitude in such cases?

149

Review of 10: 1–13

(Cf. Study 8)

150

10: 14–22 (1)

In vv. 1–13 St Paul has warned of the danger of idolatrous banquets. And he has stated that the sacraments offer no absolute safeguard against possible sin. So he argues that the sacraments make visiting such banquets a most inconsistent course of conduct There are two spiritual worlds around us, one good, one evil, and we cannot have relations with both Note these points in writing, then read these verses. v. 15 is not sarcastic.

Review Study 146, and from the material collected there explain v. 16 very carefully Note particularly that the cup after the blessing, and the bread after the breaking, are " spiritual " in themselves, like the manna and the water in vv. 3–4. Explain this fully in your own words.

The doctrine as St. Paul states it has no exact equivalent in the " classic " eucharistic theories of later times; these are all attempts to combine St. Paul's teaching with Greek philosophical conceptions Such attempts have real value, but St Paul had no interest in metaphysics.

(To give this Study its greatest value, some treatise stating the various eucharistic theories should be consulted. In these theories the religious and the philosophical elements should be distinguished carefully, the latter are only matters of human speculation)

151

10: 14–22 (2)

v. 17 is given two translations in the Revised Version, one in the text and the other in the margin. Copy the whole verse twice, once with each reading, and compare the results. In both the thought is that sharing in common food makes for unity in the participants. But scholars generally (not always, as in Moffatt's case) prefer the second version, for it is difficult to see what is meant by " we are one bread " Which version do you prefer, and why?

In any case the verse contains the doctrine known as " the table bond " On p. 817 of the Dictionary read section (b), and summarize the idea explained. Orientals feel the unifying influence of a common meal more keenly than we, although we are naturally familiar with the thought; illustrate. With bread of supernatural ("spiritual") quality, the unifying power would of course be still greater. And this power would reach its highest point in the eucharist. Explain.

I CORINTHIANS 8–11

Consequently, in any celebration of the eucharist one divine purpose is unifying the communicants, with each other as well as with God In other words, the eucharist has a *social* purpose, which is sadly neglected in our books of devotion. State this doctrine in your own words, and explain how it can be made a most profiable devotional ideal One great English bishop even insisted that we should always say " our communion," never " my communion." What do you think of his opinion?

152

10: 14–22 (3)

In v 18 what is meant by " Israel after the flesh "? What other Israel is there, and how can it be described?

Read Deuteronomy 12: 26–28, Leviticus 3: 1–5, and state the relation of sacrifices to the altar. Read Exodus 29: 35–37. This passage asserts that the altar has a " holiness " of its own by virtue of its consecration. And this " holiness " it can communicate in some degree to men, in especial (naturally) to those who eat the sacrifices (In what sense is " holiness " used here?) In a way, then, there is an analogy between the eucharist and the Jewish sacrifices; in both men come in contact with something superhuman

Consequently, St. Paul argues (vv. 19–21), it is not impossible that in idolatrous banquets men may come in contact with something diabolic. Of course, the idol in itself is of no consequence, but false worship involves worship of demons, who are of very great consequence. Hence the conclusion in v 21. The first half of v. 21 is from the Greek version of Deuteronomy 32:17; which is not the same as the Hebrew. To us the essential truth in this argument is that participation in sinful assemblies is apt to lead to sin; explain and illustrate.

v 22 is based on Deuteronomy 32:21, "Are you trying to win over God by making Him jealous? Is this safe conduct?" Explain.

Compare Moffatt's version of vv. 14–22. State the argument in your own words, and apply the thought to modern inconsistent practices.

153

10:23–11:1

In vv. 1–22 St. Paul has forbidden attendance at idolatrous banquets. He now returns to the simpler question of food merely offered to idols, and he resumes what he was saying at 8:13. Review Studies 132–133, and then read these verses. With v. 23 cf. 6:12 and the note in Study 107.

vv. 23–24 state the general principle, and its details follow. In v. 25 the "shambles" are simply the markets or shops where food (not only meat) was sold. v. 26 quotes Psalm 24:1, a common grace before meals. As the fulness of the earth belongs to the Lord, consecration to idols cannot defile it; explain.

I CORINTHIANS 8–11

Mental agitation can be avoided by asking no questions. Put vv. 25–26 into your own words. Then vv. 27, 28 and the first half of v. 29 will be clear; explain them in your own words. Can the principle of vv. 23–29a be applied to other problems? Illustrate.

vv. 29b–30 offer no special difficulty in themselves, but their connection with the context is obscure; scholars think that something has been lost from the text (Moffatt tries to avoid the difficult connection, but his paraphrase is unsatisfactory; criticize it.) The questions are those asked by the Corinthians, who objected to being controlled by other peoples' consciences. What is the proper reply?

The conclusion in 10:31–11:1 gathers up all the argument of chapters 8–10. Point out the reference of the various sentences. With 11:1 compare Philippians 3:17, and the note in Study 25.

Compare Moffatt's version.

154

Review of Chapter 10

(Cf. Study 8)

155–156

Review of Chapters 8–10

These three chapters should now be seen to form a unit. Review them, and make an outline that shows the progressive steps of the continuous argument.

157

11: 2–16 (1)

In the Greek world it was customary that respectable women should wear veils in public; the lack of a veil usually indicated low morals. But St Paul had taught the religious equality of men and women (Galatians 3: 28, etc), and the Corinthians gave practical expression to this doctrine by allowing the veils to be removed in church. This would impress outsiders very unfavorably. Read the verses. v. 2 refers to the exaggeration of St Paul's doctrine (just stated)

v 3 has been the field of endless controversy, most of it quite beside the mark. Until comparatively modern times the organization of society was generally such that woman was necessarily dependent on man. This was due to causes that no religious doctrine could affect, so that religion could only recognize existing circumstances and endeavor to ameliorate the worst evils. Much the same was true, for instance, in the recognition of the existence of arbitrary autocracy or of the institution of slavery Only centuries of evolution, not sudden religious revolution, could change these things. But, on the other hand, when society has developed so that these things are ready to disappear, it is worse than foolish to insist that we are bound by teaching produced under an entirely different state of affairs.

In other words, moral problems are of two kinds In one class, such as the worship of God, the necessity of unselfishness, etc , the laws are immutable. In the other, such as slavery, woman's position, obedience to kings, etc , the laws change with changing conditions.

State this principle very fully in your own words. Apply it concretely to the problem of woman's freedom, explaining her condition in the ancient world and the factors that have altered it today Has not the Christian spirit (even if not formal theology) played a large part in this work?

158

11 : 2–16 (2)

Realizing that in the twentieth century we are not bound by rules for the first century, no attempt should be made to soften the rather harsh teaching of this section in regard to woman's subjection.

The argument is based on Genesis 1 : 26–27, 2 · 18–24. Show how these passages help to interpret vv 7–9 (" glory " in v. 7 is used in the sense of " reflected glory "). Now this appears to explain v 10, apart from the last clause; the veil is a sign of submission to authority. How can it be interpreted in this way? Then v. 4 becomes fairly clear; for a man to veil himself would be an abdication of his independence; why? This would be especially wrong in prayer, for in prayer all our characteristics should find their truest expression; explain Then v. 5 yields the sense, " it is as unwomanly to be unveiled as it would be to wear short hair."

Rewrite vv. 3–10 (omitting the last clause of v. 10) so as to bring out the argument; this is a difficult task, and should not be hurried.

159
11 : 2–16 (3)

The last clause of v 10 is very puzzling and has many interpretations. The one most commonly supported by conservative writers is: —" The angels are present at every Christian prayer, and they watch over the behavior of the worshippers " Explain the meaning of the clause in this sense But it is right to say that there are other explanations, which need not be detailed here.

In vv 11–12 St Paul softens what he has just said It did not befit Christianity to undertake any violent change in earthly relations; the first century slave continued to serve his master, the first century wife continued in dependence on her husband. But this inferiority meant no inferiority " in the Lord," where all men are equal. Man and woman complete each other (v. 11), and, even though the first woman was made from man, all other men are born of woman (v 12). These two verses apparently contain a warning to husbands; explain them in this sense

vv. 14–15 introduce a new argument, taken from nature; the long hair indicates the necessity of further covering. Explain Does the argument seem convincing?

I CORINTHIANS 8–11

v. 16 produces still another (distinct) argument; perhaps the most convincing of all (why?). Does it perhaps indicate that St. Paul was not wholly pleased with his other reasoning?

Compare Moffatt's version.

160

11 : 2–16 (4)

Review Studies 157–159. Does the conception of the meaning of the veil in the Greek world correspond to any similar conception in modern times? In particular, does a modern woman's headcovering indicate in any way a " submission to authority "? Apart from v. 16 does anything in this section really bear on the use of a headcovering in a modern church? How does v 16 apply?

St Paul's appeal is to the commonly accepted decencies of his day, and the real kernel of his argument is found in v. 16. No community (and, still less, no individual) is called upon to overthrow harmless customs that are generally accepted. The good in such " reforms " is generally far outweighed by the disturbance and scandal caused in other people. Usually, as in the case of the veil, matters have not enough importance to be worth the energy consumed in reforming them; if we really feel called upon to start a revolution, there are plenty of real evils in the world that are worth attacking. Explain and illustrate.

161
11:17–34 (1)

vv. 2–16 are probably a comment on a sentence in the Corinthians' letter, which raised the question about the conduct of services, a theme which St. Paul now pursues in a different way. Read this section

In the Apostolic age each eucharist was made a close copy of the original institution; i e, the rite was celebrated as part of a supper (v. 21). All members of the congregation who were able brought food to be shared by all, so that no one need be hungry. In fact, those who could were supposed to eat at home, so that there would be enough for all, and so that dignity could be preserved (v. 34) At the beginning, the eucharistic bread was solemnly blessed, broken and distributed. Then the meal followed. At its close the eucharistic cup was poured, blessed and distributed. Instead of following this ceremonial, the Corinthians were divided into cliques, who ate their food in groups, without paying attention to the others Summarize these points in writing. Reread the section, and point out how this explanation applies.

162
11:17–34 (2)

vv. 18–19 have a slight tone of discouragement. "Cliques,— well, men cannot all be righteous. But the formation of cliques will show who are righteous; these will stay out of the cliques." Explain, vv 20–22 received sufficient explanation in the last Study But note that "one is hungry and another is drunken" is the sharpest possible condemnation of the lack of unity Generalize, and apply to modern times.

The recital of the Institution in vv. 23–25 is intended primarily to remind the Corinthians of the solemnity of a eucharist How does it do this? Review Study 146; it gives the fullest explanation of these verses that it seems possible to reach.

But v. 25 adds a new element, "the new covenant, established by means of Christ's blood" For the "old" covenant read Exodus 24: 1–8, copying v. 8. Explain carefully the parallel between the old and the new, noting that in the old rite the benefits of the covenant were extended to the people by sprinkling, in the new by drinking Read Hebrews 9: 11–28 (not spending too much time on obscurities), and note the points that throw further light on the present passage.

"This cup in the new covenant in my blood" is condensed to the point of obscurity. Compare St. Mark 14: 24, and reword the sentence so as to bring out the full meaning.

Compare Moffatt's version of vv. 17–25. In vv. 24–25 he has arbitrarily replaced "is" by "means."

163

11 : 17–34 (3)

v 26 is of great theological and devotional importance The broken bread, the poured out wine, taken by the people, offer a symbolic representation of the death of Christ and its benefits. Explain. This eucharistic action recalls Christ's death to the memory of the participants (cf. vv. 24-25), but it does more, it "proclaims" the fact that Christ has died for man to all who witness the action; the eucharist is a "preaching." Explain.

We may safely go a little beyond St Paul's words. The eucharistic action of course takes place in God's sight also, and so it proclaims to Him also the death of His Son for man, and pleads the benefits of this death. This is the doctrine known as the "eucharistic sacrifice"; state it in your own words. Read the Communion Office Prayer of Consecration in the Prayer Book, and show how this doctrine is utilized in our Liturgy. What is its doctrinal significance?

Attempts have been made to obtain this doctrine from vv. 24-25, by rendering "do this in memory of me" as "offer this as my memorial." This translation is universally admitted now to be impossible. And it is quite unnecessary, in view of the clear statement of the doctrine in v. 26.

In the Dictionary read the article "Eucharist," noting down the chief points.

164

11 : 17-34 (4)

v 26 is parenthetical; read vv. 23-27, omitting v. 26, and explain the connection Review the first part

I CORINTHIANS 8–11

of Study 147 By means of the manna and the water from the rock all Israelites, good and evil alike, were brought into contact with heavenly gifts; how is it in the Eucharist? Explain v. 27 accordingly. (Note that in the Apostolic ritual the passing of the cup followed the passing of the bread at a considerable interval, hence St. Paul's "or"; a man might fall into sin in the meantime) Explain vv. 28–29 "Discern" is an excellent translation, but "recognize the presence of" comes nearer the sense

Careless contact with holy things is fearfully dangerous; explain how v. 30 can be illustrated by I Samuel 5 St Paul means literally that God may punish an irreverent communion by physical weakness; this is quite conceivable, but what other forms is the punishment more likely to take? How does, "Never make a communion without self-examination," explain v. 31? In v 32 St. Paul softens the reproof a little "When God punishes us it is to warn us to correct our ways, that we may not be condemned." Compare Hebrews 12: 4–13, and explain the connection.

Compare Moffatt's version of vv. 26–34

165

Review of 11: 17–34

(Cf. Study 8)

166

Write a complete description of St. Paul's eucharistic doctrine, based on the material collected in Studies 146, 150–153, 161–164. Note especially that it was regarded as a joyous feast, capable of degenerating into such abuses as the drunkenness of 11:21.

Note. Such abuses towards the end of the Apostolic age caused the eucharist to be separated from the accompanying supper, and to be transferred to the early morning. The supper by itself was continued (or was revived) under the title "Agape," or "Love Feast."

167–168

Review of Studies 130–166

(Cf. Studies 31–32)

169

Review of Chapters 8–11

(Cf. Study 8)

170

Review your work in Studies 92 and 129. How does the further study in chapters 8–11 supplement the conclusions drawn?

SECTION VI

I CORINTHIANS 12–14

171

Review Studies 69, 70, 96 and 130 Read chapters 12–14, and paragraph 8 on p. 158 of the Dictionary Extend your outline to cover chapters 12–14.

172

12: 1–3

Read these verses, noting that they take up another question of the Corinthians. Note that in v. 1 the word " gifts " is in italics, indicating that it has been supplied by the translators The Greek may mean " concerning spiritual *persons*," with " spiritual " much in the sense of 10: 3–4, " persons with supernatural endowments " Review Study 148 rapidly.

v. 2 describes a phenomenon common in the Gentile world The idols were " dumb," but their votaries were not. Very frequently in idolatrous worship persons would lose all self-control, and would be carried away into hysteria, uttering all kinds of outcries. And persons in this state were usually thought to be inspired. Compare Acts 16: 16–18, and explain how it illustrates this verse. Expand this verse in your own language, so as to describe the phenomenon in modern terms

The theme of v. 2 is continued in v. 3, the wild self-abandon of heathendom reappeared among converts to Christianity also, and in hysteria shocking blasphemies were sometimes uttered. ("Anathema" means simply "accursed") Such occurrences perplexed the church; as these persons were inspired, how could such utterances be explained? St. Paul, in effect, replies, "It may be a spirit that inspires them, but not the spirit of God" Review Study 59. What test does St. Paul make of the nature of the Spirit speaking? Compare I St. John 4: 1-3; what light does it throw on the present passage? What test does St John make? Why is it more elaborate than St. Paul's (note that it was written fifty years later)?

Write a description of a meeting of Apostolic Christians, in which such ecstatic phenomena both true and false) occurred. Just what information did the Corinthians seek from St Paul?

Compare Moffatt's version, noting that his rendition of v. 2 can be improved.

173

12: 4-11 (1)

Review Study 172. The Corinthians were interested chiefly in the various types of religious ecstasy;

I CORINTHIANS 12-14

so St. Paul begins by warning them that ecstasy is only one form of God's gifts. Read these verses. Note very carefully the Trinitarian parallelism in vv 4–7. Is the distinction between the operations of the Three Persons real or only rhetorical? Explain carefully In v. 8 " to profit withal " should be " for the common good " No spiritual gift has a selfish purpose. Explain

Make a list of the seven gifts of the Spirit enumerated in vv 8–10, and a similar list of the nine gifts enumerated in v 28. What terms are common to these lists? Make a list of the seven gifts in Romans 12 6–8. Note that " prophecy " is the only term common to all three lists. Does it seem that any of these lists is meant to be at all formal or exhaustive?

The distinction between " wisdom " and " knowledge " in v. 9 is clearly meant to be real, but the meanings of the English words do not give the precise distinction " Wisdom " is explained very abundantly in chapters 1–2; review them briefly and write a definition of the word in its good sense " Knowledge " is probably less philosophical and mystical, dealing more with practical problems. Explain and illustrate.

174

12 4–11 (2)

Review Study 173 All Christians are supposed to have faith, but faith can also reach such extraordinary heights as to be a special gift of God (v. 9). Presumably special power in prayer is meant. Compare St. Mark 9:23, 11:22–24, St. Matthew 17:19–20, St. Luke 17:5–6, and explain the term. What are "gifts of healing"?

Note that all the gifts thus far are non-ecstatic; the more wondrous gifts begin in v 10. Why does St. Paul so guard against giving "spiritual" (v. 1) the quality of the merely extraordinary?

"Miracles" in v. 10 does not include "healings" (v. 9), but it does include (perhaps chiefly) the casting out of evil spirits. "Prophecy" is the most important term of all. In the Dictionary read the article "Prophet (in NT)" very carefully, noting down the chief points Define the term briefly. By reference to Study 172 explain "discerning of spirits." "Tongues" and "the interpretation of tongues" will be considered later.

Why does v. 11 repeat v. 4 with such emphasis? Compare Moffatt's version.

175

12:12–21

This famous passage requires little explanation. It was written to guard against pride and jealousy; in particular, it discourages vanity in the possession of the more showy gifts. Read the verses, and state the argument in your own terms, with reference to modern conditions

Compare Moffatt's version

In the Dictionary read the article "Spiritual Gifts" and note down the chief points

176

12: 22–26

Review the first part of Study 175, and then read vv. 12–26 as a continuous whole. In vv. 22–26 the figure becomes a little more obscure. Explain v 22; the eye would be an example of a "feeble" part (St Paul is not thinking of the internal organs) Contrast the functions and qualifications of the eye and (say) the hand, and apply the contrast to two vocations in the Church.

The thought in v. 23 is a little fanciful The parts of the body that are "less honorable" (no specific parts are meant) have the "honor" of clothing, while the "honorable" parts must go bare Explain this in your own words In the application the fancifulness disappears Weaker souls have a claim to courtesy and protection, which more independent natures must do without E g , does not every one at times long to be a child again? Illustrate more fully.

Explain vv. 24–25 A slight amputation may leave the body still fairly efficient, but it is no longer perfect. And God wills the perfection of the Church in all her members. In v 26 St. Paul is thinking only of the Church, not of the human body; why? Compare the ideal set forth in this verse with the actualities of today. How can improvement be begun?

Review Study 151 rapidly.
Compare Moffatt's version.

177

12 : 27–31

St Paul comes finally to the direct application of the figure worked out so elaborately. Read these verses. Review Studies 173–174 carefully. Here the list of gifts begins with the title of the three most important offices in the primitive Church For "Apostle" review Study 136; write a short definition. Were the Apostles local or general officers of the Church? How was "prophet" defined in Study 174? Copy Acts 11:27, 13:1–3, 15:32, 21:9–10. Were the prophets local or general officers of the Church, or both? Note the close connection of "Apostles" and "prophets" in Ephesians 2·20, 3:5, 4:11; together they made up the primary sources of revelation; explain (An Apostle might, of course, be a prophet also)

The "teachers" differed from the prophets in not possessing direct inspiration; cf. v. 8. How do II St. Timothy 2:2, 3:14–17 throw light on their office? Define "teacher" in your own terms. They were usually local officials.

What offices would "helps" probably describe? "Governments" is interesting; the disciplinary and business management of a church was not usually committed to the "teachers." Compare Ephesians

4: 11, where "pastors" are likewise distinguished from "teachers." Are teaching and business gifts generally found in the same person? Note that in the Apostolic age the endowments of a vestryman would be considered a spiritual gift. Is not this the correct point of view?

Ephesians 4: 11 also names "evangelists," travelling missionaries of a rank below that of the Apostles.

v. 31 closes the argument; explain it. Does this verse forbid us to be content when God gives only a lesser gift?

Compare Moffatt's version

178

Review Studies 58, 177, and the lists drawn up in Study 173. When the intense miraculous activity of the Spirit ceased, which of these offices (and gifts) necessarily disappeared (give the reason in each case)?

The chief functions of the Apostles were bearing witness to Christ from personal knowledge, founding churches (this included choosing the ministers) and exercising authority over these churches. Which of these functions are possessed by bishops? What other functions are possessed by bishops?

How in the modern Church is the gift of teaching distributed? Properly qualified laymen can be licensed to give addresses in church; is this just? And any teaching that is at all officially recognized (even by a Sunday School appointment) comes under the "gift" of teaching; explain   What responsibility does such a gift confer?

Where is the gift of "government" found in the modern Church? The gift of "help"? How do laymen share in such gifts?

St. Paul does not explain how the right to administer the sacraments was distributed, but the prophets certainly had special recognition in this regard. What Apostolic offices are combined in the modern priesthood? In the modern diaconate? Has either of these offices still other prerogatives?

In the Dictionary the article "Ministry" may be read rapidly (more carefully, if time permits).

179

Review of Chapter 12

(Cf. Study 8)

180

Chapter 13

This perfect chapter is universally recognized as St. Paul's masterpiece. Read it through, and then reread it, noting carefully the divisions in the thought.

Review Study 135 rapidly; at first sight chapter 9 seemed a digression, but it really forms an important link between chapters 8 and 10. Just so chapter 13 occupies an important place between chapters 12 and 14; the Corinthians were disposed to prize the more showy gifts, at the expense of love. Reread the chapter, and make a list of the points that bear on this argument

181

13:1–3

The King James Version uses "charity" in place of "love" throughout this chapter; why is this rendition highly unfortunate in modern English? To us it is a bad translation; the Greek uses the ordinary word for "love," and that for "charity" is entirely different.

Show in detail how vv. 1–2 take up 12:8–10. The gift of tongues was highly ecstatic and extremely audible (cf. Acts 2:4–6), and without love it degenerates into mere noise. So a modern revival can work up individuals into a state of wild hysteria, without doing any real spiritual good. Explain and illustrate more fully. Treat each of the statements in vv 1–3 similarly.

The verdict on "faith" in v. 2 is puzzling; why? But persons sometimes have a reputation for powers they do not possess; would this explain the difficulty?

Compare Moffatt's version.

182

13:4–7 (1)

Read these verses, and compare Moffatt's version carefully The latter gives all the explanation required. Illustrate each of St. Paul's statements with a concrete example.

183

13:4–7 (2)

Write a general definition of "love" in the modern sense of the term, making it rather full. Compare this definition with St Paul's (in the present passage) and note the differences Note especially that St. Paul has nothing to say about the *emotional* side of "love"; is it not possible to display all the qualities enumerated without feeling the least emotional attraction towards the person in question? Write a careful distinction between service that proceeds from emotional affection and service that proceeds from a sense of duty; which does St. Paul commend? Read St. Luke 6: 32–35; how does it bear on the question? Is "natural" love (even mother love) in itself a quality that inevitably leads towards God? Illustrate how such love may lead to evil. How is it distinguished, then, from Christian love?

184

13:8–13

Read these verses; the contrast throughout is between this world and the next. In v. 8 "never faileth" means simply "shall never cease." In heaven there will be no need of tongues, prophecy or knowledge; explain. How does v. 9 supplement your explanation? How does v. 11 carry on the argument? Note how St. Paul deprecates the Corinthians' love of display as "childish"; explain.

I CORINTHIANS 12–14

The ancient mirrors (v. 12) were of polished metal, and the cheaper sort were poor reflectors. So the "darkness" ("indistinctness") of the image was a familiar annoyance. "We know something of heaven already, but our knowledge is like the imperfect reflection in a mirror." Explain the second half of this verse.

In v 13 "now" refers to the life of heaven, in which there will still exist faith and hope as well as love. The thought seems strange at first sight (what familiar hymn asserts the precise opposite?), but it is intentional. Even with the fullness of heavenly knowledge (v. 12), will our acquaintance with God be so infinite that nothing is left for faith? Shall we not always be glad to serve Him without knowing every reason? Nor is the heavenly life mere quiescence; it grows continually, and we grow with it Hence will not both faith and hope have a part, as we look towards the future? Write a little meditation on heaven, that brings out St. Paul's point.

Note once more the practical aim of this chapter, love is greater than any " spiritual gift." How does this bear on the argument in chapter 12?

Compare Moffatt's version.

185

Review of Chapter 13

(Cf. Study 8)

186–187

In the Dictionary review the article "Spiritual Gifts," and then read the article, "Tongues, Gift of" very carefully, noting down the points in full and writing out all the Biblical references

188

The following definition of "tongues" may be adopted. An ecstatic state, in which the speaker loses self-control, and screams out words that are ordinarily unintelligible. Sometimes they may be scraps or sentences from a foreign language, sometimes they may be mere gibberish Copy this definition. What modern parallels can be found, where religious emotionalism is at its height (reckless revivals, etc)? The value of "tongues" is the value of the ability to rise to heights of unrestrained religious emotion? Before studying St. Paul's discussion of this gift state your own estimate of it rather fully.

Read chapter 14 and note the correspondence of its statements with the definition of "tongues" above.

189

14: 1–5

Read these verses. The quiet virtue, "love," is not technically a "spiritual gift," although it is higher than any of them, but the Christian should endeavor to be as many sided as possible Cf. 12: 31 and write a brief note on "Christian ambition." Why is prophecy the highest of all the "gifts" (vv. 4–5)?

Does v. 2 imply that the "tongues" as practiced in Corinth were foreign languages or unintelligible sounds? Note that in 12:10 "interpretation of tongues" is classed among the "gifts"; would ability to interpret a foreign language normally be a "gift" or a natural accomplishment? What would be the case with ability to interpret unintelligible ecstasy? Was the ability to interpret often found (v 28)? A speaker sometimes had the gift himself (v. 5); does this seem to have been usual?

Note that in v. 2 "mysteries" has the modern sense; contrast 2:7 and the explanation in Study 78.

State the argument of this section in your own words, so as to be easily intelligible to the modern reader.

Compare Moffatt's version.

190

14 · 6–12

Review Study 189, and note carefully the emphasis in vv 1–5 on the *social* value of the Christian virtues; that virtue is the highest that offers the greatest good for the whole Church Explain and illustrate, contrasting the value of emotional and of "practical" religion in the present day. Apply the results to v. 6. Note the repetition in this verse, " revelation "—" prophesying," " knowledge "—" teaching." Read vv. 7–9

138 THE TEACHINGS OF ST PAUL

and explain the argument, how does it apply to the "tongues"?

Read vv 10–11 The translation of v 10 is not very clear, the sense is, "There are, doubtless, ever so many languages in the world" These two verses do not describe the "tongues" directly, they are an illustration taken from languages, just as vv 7–9 are an illustration taken from music What is the meaning of "barbarian" in v 11? Explain the two verses

In v 12 substitute the marginal reading for the one in the text There is of course only one Spirit, but St Paul uses (ironically) the current language of the heathen world Explain the rebuke in the choice of these words, which suggest division rather than unity

Compare Moffatt's version

191

14 13–19 (1)

Read these verses With v. 13 cf v. 5 and the note in Study 189

v 14 contains a very important religious truth To all intents, "spirit" here is the emotional side of man's nature (the Holy Spirit is not at all implied). A person may feel intense emotional enthusiasm, while his intellect is untouched Explain at length, and give several illustrations, the importance of this theme warrants devoting special time to it Explain vv 15–16, noting that ecstasy was especially likely to occur in the midst of a thanksgiving

I CORINTHIANS 12–14

For "the unlearned" in v 16 cf. v 23, where this class is distinguished from "the whole church" on the one hand, and from "unbelievers" on the other Evidently they were converts under instruction, who had not yet accepted baptism That a special "place" was reserved for them is interesting, note that they were expected to say "Amen" at the close of the prayers Believers might have experience enough to know what a speaker "with tongues" was trying to say, but the unlearned would be baffled

How does the principle thus laid down bear on the use of dead languages in the public services of the Church? How does it bear on the use of versions of the Scripture written in obsolete English? Can you suggest any reforms needed in our own Church?

192

14: 13–19 (2)

Review Study 191 In vv 17–18 St Paul introduces a little safeguard "I do not mean that 'tongues' are worthless; far from it. A thanksgiving that rises to ecstasy is a good thanksgiving, and I rejoice that I have the gift myself" Emotion is good, but uncontrolled emotional display is for private, not public, edification. This principle includes more than ecstasy E g, many persons nowadays find their devotion greatly helped by ritual practices, etc, which are not always understood or liked by the congregation in which they worship Illustrate What should be the rule for such persons? Write a short note on "devotional selfishness."

Compare Moffatt's version. In vv. 16 and 23 " outsider " is not a good translation; " learner " or " candidate " would be much better.

Review your paper on religious emotion written in Study 188 Does your research since then indicate any modifications?

193
Review of 14: 1–19
(Cf. Study 8)

194
14: 20–25 (1)

Read these verses Restate v 20 so as to bring out the idea more clearly; " children as regards evil, men as regards mind " An exaggerated love for the merely showy is rebuked; cf. 13: 11 and explain.

vv. 21–22 are another instance of a Rabbinical use of the Old Testament, which we find difficult to understand. Compare Isaiah 28·11–13; does St. Paul seem to give the general sense of this passage? In the first half of v. 22 " sign " is meant in a special sense. A display of God's power is usually meant to bring men to repentance (read the Dictionary article " Sign "), but such means only make hardened sinners worse Compare Exodus 10: 1–3, St Luke 2: 34–35 and show their relation to the present passage v. 23 explains more fully; in " tongues " there is a display of God's power, which unbelievers will mock as madness. How does this make the "tongues" a sign? Give modern instances of such "signs," which involve the mockery of good things by unbelievers who refuse to understand them   Compare St. Matthew 7:6, how does it apply?

Generally speaking, we should avoid giving such "signs" to unbelievers. This is St Paul's advice; illustrate   But at times it is impossible to avoid a crisis; men cannot always be spared making a final decision. Compare St Luke 19:41-44; Our Lord knew He would be rejected, but He could not avoid giving the "sign."

One danger of postponing repentance is the certainty that in time repentance will become impossible, when God's signs only serve to harden. Explain and illustrate.

195

14:20-25 (2)

The second clause of v. 22 is so obscure that most experts confess their inability to understand it. Judging from the first clause, what ought the meaning to be? But, unless the force of "sign" is entirely changed, does a "sign for believers" make sense? And what difficulty is there in reconciling this clause with vv 24-25? Either St. Paul has expressed himself very carelessly, or there is something wrong with the text.

vv. 24-25 throw an interesting light on the nature

of prophecy. St Paul does not mean that the prophets were actually inspired to read the thoughts of strangers, in fact, the prophets would not address the strangers directly But the prophets' ability to touch men's consciences in revealing God's will would make the stranger think that his thoughts were being read Is not this a common experience in listening to a great preacher? Illustrate Note St Paul's point very carefully; the Christian's knowledge of moral truth should be so intense that any responsive conscience will be affected Explain and illustrate

Note that even the earliest Christian meetings were freely open to outsiders; probably even the celebrations of the eucharist, during which the greatest spiritual manifestations would occur.

Omitting v 22b, state the argument of vv. 20–25 in your own words

Compare Moffatt's version. Compare the note on v 26 The quotation in v 25 is from Isaiah 45:14 (verify it).

196

14.26–33a (1)

Read these verses In v 26 the only new term is "psalm"; a song of praise composed especially for the occasion, on the model of the Psalter Compare Ephesians 5 19, where there is little distinction between the three kinds of sacred poetry named Specimens of early Christian hymns can be found in Revelation (5·9, 12, 13, 7.10, etc), in the Dictionary read the article "Hymn," and note down the chief points Write brief definitions of the other terms in v. 26 The inspiration to give an "interpretation" would of course not be felt until someone had spoken in a "tongue."

vv 27–28 are self-explanatory; "if no one is present who is known to have the gift of interpretation, he who feels an impulse to speak in a 'tongue' must control himself" Draw a picture of the confusion that would result if these directions were violated

v 29 is clear, "two or three sermons at one service are generally enough!" The "others" are the other prophets, who are to keep watch lest false inspiration appear (cf 12.3, and the note in Study 172). The case in v 30 would not be likely to arise unless the first speaker grew tedious, why do the directions in vv 29–30 have something amusing in them? v. 31 addresses the prophets only; why? Of course "all can prophesy" means "at one service or another," not "all at the same service" Did Corinthian customs need reform?

v 32 contains a highly important rule, "if a man is a true prophet, he can subject his spirit and keep silence", explain. Explain all of vv 32–33a

Compare Moffatt's version.

197
14: 26–33a (2)

Review Study 196 Write, as concretely as possible, a description of an early Christian service, from the standpoint of a stranger, telling just what he would have seen and heard; assume that an "interpreter" was present, and that speaking with "tongues" occurred.

Note carefully that the outpouring of enthusiasm was due to the youth of the Church. Such enthusiasm cannot be long maintained, and it can be revived only under great stimulus and for short periods. Illustrate. This is no evil, faithful quiet service is just as holy as high enthusiasm. To be sure the waning of enthusiasm brought a certain loss, but there were compensating gains; explain and illustrate.

Should modern worship endeavor to conform to the ideals of an earlier period, or should they express the actual facts of modern life (in so far as these facts are good)? Cite some modern instances of attempts to copy early enthusiasm, which have soon settled into an orderly routine. Do liturgical services, consequently, need any apology? How can enthusiasm find its proper outlet?

198

14: 33*b*–40

Omitting vv. 33*b*–35, read vv. 26–40 as a continuous whole. Note that the omission causes no break. vv. 36–38 contain a sharp rebuke of devotional selfishness. The translation of v 38 is uncertain, but the variations do not matter much; perhaps, "If any one is ignorant, let him be ignored." Explain the three verses. How do vv. 39–40 sum up the argument?

I CORINTHIANS 12-14

Compare Moffatt's version of vv. 33b–40.
Note that he prints vv. 33b–36 at the end; compare his footnote. (It is hardly necessary to move v. 36.) Explain the meaning of these verses by themselves. Now compare 11:4, does there seem to be a conflict? Some scholars, accordingly, think that these verses were written in the margin of a manuscript of this Epistle at a later time, when the subsidence of "enthusiasm" gave women no longer any reason for speaking in church. This marginal note was then copied by accident into the text of the Epistle.

Unquestionably the copying in of marginal notes ("glosses") has occasionally (but very rarely) happened elsewhere; the most famous instance is in I St. John 5:7 (compare the King James Version with the Revised Version). Does this theory seem reasonable here? Would you be inclined to accept it?

199

Review of Chapter 14

(Cf Study 8)

200–201

Review of Studies 171–199

(Cf. Studies 31–32)

202

Review of Chapters 12–14

(Cf Study 8)

203-204

Compare the argument in chapters 12-14 with the argument in chapters 8-10, showing how in both cases St Paul starts from the same principle, that of the greatest good to the greatest number. Note how the same principle is worked out in Romans 14. This principle is basic in all problems of Christian conduct; it is simply the application of St. Matthew 22 39 (explain). And it is the counterpoise to our other great principle, that of Christian liberty. In themselves, such questions as, "May I speak with 'tongues'?", "May I eat things offered to idols?", "Need I make food distinctions?", are matters that each may settle as he pleases. But the extent to which such pleasure should be carried depends on our influence on others

State this antithesis between social relations and liberty in your own words. Take some current problems of personal conduct, and endeavor to treat them as St Paul would have done

205

Review your work in Studies 92, 129, and 170. How does the further study in chapters 12-14 supplement the conclusions drawn?

SECTION VII

I CORINTHIANS 15–16

206

Review Studies 69, 70, 96, 130, and 171   Read chapters 15–16, and paragraph 9 on p 158 of the Dictionary   Extend your outline to cover chapters 15–16.

207–208

As a preparation for a close study of chapter 15, make outlines of St. Matthew 28; St. Mark 16: 1–8 and 19–20 (separately), St Luke 24, St John 20–21, giving the facts about each Resurrection appearance of Our Lord (when? where? before whom? what was said? etc)   But it is hardly advisable to attempt to unite these outlines into a continuous account; this would require very special and detailed study.

209

On pp 456–458 of the Dictionary, read the section " The Resurrection," noting down the chief points. Study this section carefully

210

15: 1–11 (1)

Read these verses Which of the appearances in vv. 4–7 can be identified with the lists drawn up from the Gospels? Which appearances here are not related in the Gospels?

Read v. 11 again. Note carefully that St. Paul gives only such appearances as were attested by the direct experience of apostolic *preachers*. Which appearances in the Gospels does St. Paul omit because they do not come under this description (e g., did St. Mary Magdalene preach?)

In v. 7 what is the meaning of "all the apostles" (Study 136)?

Note that in St Paul's list there are three groups of many witnesses (which are they?) What is the special force of such testimony? What value has the evidence in v. 8 (remember that to St. Paul his conversion was a fearfully serious matter)? What is the cumulative force of all the testimony adduced?

211

15: 1–11 (2)

Write a definition of Christ's Resurrection, explaining how it differs from the resuscitation of (say) Lazarus, or the blessed life in heaven (say) Abraham. Note that the essential fact is that Christ arose to *both* earth and heaven. He returned to His own and to

I CORINTHIANS 15-16

God's right hand simultaneously (if we neglect the distinction between the Resurrection and the Ascension). Lazarus came back only to earth, Abraham went only to heaven, but Christ's Resurrection is defined by His title "Lord." Explain this in detail; it is of the utmost importance. Read St John 14: 19-21, 27-29, 16: 19-22, and show how these passages confirm the doctrine just stated.

212

15: 1-11 (3)

The theme of chapter 15 is stated in v. 12. Probably some Corinthians were content to hold the Greek doctrine of a mere immortality of the soul, a doctrine that St Paul regarded as incomplete, because it left man incomplete. Explain. He replies, "A resurrection is not impossible, for in Christ's case it has already happened!" But note that the Corinthians did not doubt Christ's resurrection; vv. 1-11 are meant as a reminder, not as a proof (what is the difference?) "In doubting the possibility of a resurrection, you seem to have forgotten that Christ rose." Compare Moffatt's version of vv 1-2 State these two verses in your own terms

Why is St Paul so emphatic in recalling to them the original form of his message? Cf. Galatians 1: 8-9; there is only one basis for historic Christianity, the doctrine taught by the Apostles.

In v. 3 how does St. Paul say, "This is not my own

invention"? But compare Galatians 1·11–12; does there seem to be a contradiction? In reality there is no contradiction, the historic facts about Christ's life St Paul learned from other men, and he passed these facts on unchanged But the interpretation of these facts (the "Gospel" in Galatians) he learned directly by Christ's inspiration; distinguish between the two meanings of "Gospel" So in Christianity always there is a permanent element, but this may lead to new interpretations when confronted with new circumstances Explain carefully, and illustrate How can we preserve a balance between rigid conservatism and pure radicalism? What are the dangers of each?

213

15·1–11 (4)

A "creed" is a formula for recitation; do vv 3–4 form a creed in this sense? But do they not imply everything that a creed implies? Was the Apostolic age without fixed dogma?

In v. 4 note the word "buried"; what sense does it give "hath been raised"? Is it compatible with the belief that only Christ's spirit appeared to the disciples? In v 8 "untimely born" is an insult thrown at St Paul by his enemies, compare Moffatt's renditions, and explain the insult Can v 9 also be understood as a charge against St Paul? If so, St. Paul admits its truth, and then replies in v. 10; note his humility. Review Study 136 and explain why he says what he does in v. 10.

v. 11 insists again on fidelity to tradition here; "in some doctrines I have received unique revelation, but in this we all agree." Why is he so emphatic?

Compare Moffatt's version.

214

Review of 15: 1–11

(Cf. Study 8)

215

15: 12–19

Read these verses. The arguments are of three kinds. v. 18 shows that belief in the resurrection is desirable, v. 15 appeals to St. Paul's sincerity, the other arguments are based on religious experience. Explain the difference. Which is the most important?

v. 15 deserves special attention. However attractive a religious belief may be, if it is not true it is false witness against God. Is this principle often forgotten? In any matter of importance is it right to say, "I *like* to believe it"? Is it well to say this even in unimportant matters? Illustrate the great harm (both to one's self and to others) that can come from violating this principle. What guarantee does St. Paul's candor give us of the care he has used in investigating the evidence for the Resurrection of Christ? How is this important to us?

What is the validity of the argument in v 14? Review Study 211 and answer this question carefully Would a belief that Christ is Lord satisfy our faith, apart from a belief in His physical Resurrection? Give your reasons fully

v. 17 is often slurred. "If Christ has not been raised, the Law is still in force and we are under its condemnation"; state this in your own words v 19 depends partly on v. 17, "if the Law is still in force, we can have no hope after death." Explain. But the verse contains also a more general sense; explain and illustrate.

Compare Moffatt's version.

216

15 : 20–22

Read these verses. The thought is developed more at length in Romans 5 : 12–21; read this passage and compare Moffatt's version of it. Draw up a table showing the correspondence between Adam and Christ, and a second table showing their differences In the Dictionary read the article "Adam in the NT," and note down the chief points. Read also the article "Adam," and note down the chief points Explain carefully how the writer reconciles the story in Genesis with the evolutionary theory. Is this reconciliation satisfactory?

217

On pp. 691–693 of the Dictionary read paragraphs 2–5. Note down the chief points, especially as they apply to the present discussion.

218–219

15 : 23–24

Review Studies 101–103 carefully. Read these verses, noting that they contain three stages, "Christ the first fruits,— then — then — ." The second stage is the beginning of the Millennium. Explain the two verses accordingly in your own terms. In the Dictionary read the articles "Millennium" and "Chiliasm." Note down the chief points, and criticize these articles.

For the "first fruits" read Leviticus 23 · 9–21, and summarize the ceremonial of the rite; this feast was kept before the general harvest began. Why, then, does St. Paul speak of Our Lord as the "first fruits"?

220

15 : 25–28

Read these verses, and explain vv. 25–26 from the Millennium doctrine Compare St Paul's teaching with that in Revelation 20 : 1–10 St Paul represents the Millennial reign as a continual progress of victory for Christ, who subdues one enemy after another, until He finally destroys death. This brings about the general resurrection (why?), and the Kingdom is then ready to be delivered to the Father. How does St John's picture differ from this? Why have these divergences not the slightest importance for our faith?

The pronouns in vv 27–28 are very confusing, rewrite these verses without using pronouns. "Son" here does not mean "God the Son," it means simply "Messiah," an office of Christ's *human* nature. At the end we shall not need the mediation even of the Sacred Humanity of Our Lord; we shall view God directly. Compare I St John 3:2 and explain how it illustrates this passage. Is there anything irreverent in saying that Christ as Man will become subject to the Father (St. John 14·28)? State these two verses in your own words.

Compare Moffatt's version.

221

15:29–34

Read these verses. Many curious interpretations have been proposed of v. 29, but the simplest meaning is much the best; some Corinthians had instituted a practice of having themselves baptized for the benefit of deceased persons (probably those whom death had deprived of the sacrament.) Such rites were common in heathenism, and they evidently were carried temporarily into Christianity by converts who had been accustomed to them. Did such a practice do any particular harm? Was there any special reason for St. Paul to interfere? Yet could such a rite do any real good? Was not the Church wise in suppressing it afterwards? Irregularities may be sometimes tolerated, which should be forbidden as permanent institutions; illustrate. What doctrine of baptism did the Corinthian practice presuppose? How would it support St. Paul's argument for the resurrection?

vv. 30–32 are a unit. "Die" in v. 31 means "run into mortal danger." St. Paul swears ("protests") by something very sacred to him, his pride in the Corinthians. Explain, noting the tact. The "beasts" in verse 32 were vicious men. Acts 19:23–34 (read the passage) happened after I Corinthians was written, but it illustrates the present verse admirably (how?) State vv. 30–32 in your own words. The second clause of v. 33 is from a Greek poet, and is in meter. These "evil companionships" had led to a denial of the resurrection.

The second clause of v. 34 is sarcastic; cf. 8:1 and explain the sarcasm.

Compare Moffatt's version.

222

Review of 15:1–34

(Cf. Study 8)

223

15: 35-44a

Read these verses The resurrection body differs from our present body, but this does not affect the truth of the resurrection.

In v. 36 "die" means only "is buried"; does a seed really die in this case? In v. 38 note that St Paul uses "pleased," not "pleases"; at the time of creation God determined just what kind of "body" each seed should have. Explain the illustration. How does v. 39 continue the argument?

In modern English what does "celestial bodies" mean? But in v. 40 this phrase means "bodies of celestial beings"; note that these bodies are not said to have "flesh" (why not?) Have terrestrial bodies any real "glory"?

Earthly bodies are of different sorts (v. 29), celestial bodies differ from these (v. 40) and from one another (v. 41) as well; how does this help St. Paul's argument? Does v. 41 suggest that St. Paul conceived of the sun, etc., as angelic powers? Would the illustration help his argument otherwise? Is there any reason to suppose he had any scientific knowledge of the true nature of the sun? Would revelation have informed him on this subject? Has the matter any practical importance?

Show how vv. 42-44a sum up the argument. Review Study 146. The difference between "natural" and "spiritual" is well indicated in v. 40; note that the sun (e g.) is "spiritual" and not "natural"; why?

Compare Moffatt's version.

224

15: 44b–49

Read these verses Review Study 216.

This section is more difficult than appears at first sight, for it refers to a belief held among the Jews. Read Genesis 1:27 and compare it with Genesis 2:7 (quoted in v. 45 here) From these two verses some Jews deduced that there were two Adams, one "spiritual" (1:27), one "natural" (2:7). How could such an opinion be reached? So v. 46 is a protest against this teaching; note that "is" here refers to earthly appearance, not to creation (why?) Explain the use of "spiritual." Explain v 47

Returning to v. 45, it should be observed that in Greek "soul" means "naturalness" here, and the term is derogatory, "only a 'natural' soul." (The play on words is almost impossible to reproduce in English; compare Moffat's attempt) Christ was (of course) always a "life giving spirit," but St. Paul thinks of the special life giving power of the Ascension Explain the verse. Does its second sentence seem to be quoted? If so, St. Paul is citing some lost writing

There are two Adams, each with children of a like nature; explain v 48. Now go back to v 44b. The logic is this:—"Every descendant of an Adam has a body like this Adam's; hence, as children of the natural Adam inherit a natural body, the children of the spiritual Adam must inherit a spiritual body." v. 48 applies this general truth to ourselves. The whole argument may be summarized, "As we now derive our life from Christ, our resurrection body shall be like Christ's."

Review the section slowly, making sure you understand it. In the Dictionary read paragraph (*a*) on p. 707.

Compare Moffatt's version.

225

15 : 50–53 (1)

Read these verses. The first half of v. 50 uses Jewish terms, the second half Greek; explain

Review Study 51, and compare its teaching with that of vv 51–52. In v. 51 what is the meaning of " mystery "?

The idea in v. 53 finds fuller expression in II Corinthians 5 : 1–5; read this section and compare Moffatt's version. St. Paul compares his body to a " tent," which is not permanent, and he desires his heavenly body, his eternal " home " And he hopes that the new body will come while he is yet alive, so that death will not leave him " naked " (without any body at all). Rewrite this passage in your own words without using the figurative expressions Show how it explains v. 53.

226

15: 50–53 (2)

Review Study 225. The passage is extremely interesting, for it shows why St Paul thought immortality of the soul alone to be unsatisfactory; it is a "naked" state. Explain Is his conception plausible? Yet even a disembodied soul can be happier than any one in the present body; read II Corinthian 5: 6–10 (compare Moffatt's version) To be "with the Lord" makes up and more than makes up for having no body; cf. Philippians 1:23, and explain its bearing here.

Stripped of Jewish terminology, St Paul teaches that between death and the resurrection the righteous are with Christ in happiness, but their nature will be complete only at the end Until the consummation we shall always lack something.

Is the Christian hope for mere individual blessedness, or for a Kingdom, a City? Explain the difference between these concepts. Consequently, can our own nature be made wholly full, when the Divine Society is still incomplete? And this Society can be organized only when history is complete (why?) And a "body" is eminently the means through which we express social relationships; explain Show, therefore, that St Paul's expectation of a heavenly

160　THE TEACHINGS OF ST. PAUL

body only at the end of time is bound up intimately with the social nature of Christianity.

Read the paragraph "Eschatology" on p 694 of the Dictionary Does it suggest anything new?

227

15·50–53 (3)

Review Studies 225–226 We have now this question to consider, "What continuity does St. Paul assume between our present body and the resurrection body?"

In II Corinthians 5:1–2 where does the resurrection body come from? How is this heavenly origin confirmed by the term "spiritual body" in I Corinthians 15:44? In the case of a person alive at the end, how is "clothed upon" in II Corinthians 5:2–3 to be explained? How does I Corinthians 15:53 confirm this language? Is the following statement a fair representation of St Paul's thought:—"The resurrection body descends from heaven over our present body, if we are still alive, and swallows it up"? Does this heavenly body, then, continue or replace our present body?

But, as a matter of fact, scientists tell us that the material in our present bodies changes completely every seven years; does the new material continue or replace the old? Yet we say that we have the *same* body through our whole life; what do we mean by "same"? A body is mine because it is the medium through which my intelligence acts; does this definition seem fair? Must there, then, be continuity of *material* between our present body and our resurrection body? Need the destruction of the material of a dead body (by fire, etc.) affect belief in the resurrection?

But, it should be said, these questions imply answers that carry us further than St Paul's words. Review Study 107. It will be seen there that a continuity *of some kind* is assumed between the present body and the resurrection body, although 6:13 tells against this being a continuity of material. Would the fact that both bodies have the same soul satisfy the requirement of sameness? Scholars are entirely at variance; state what you think. Does Philippians 3:20-21 throw any additional light?

228

15·54-58

Read these verses. Explain the first half of v 54 from the principles discussed in Study 227. Verify the quotations from Isaiah 25:8 and Hosea 13·14; has St Paul kept the original sense?

v 56 carries us into a part of St Paul's teaching which he discusses at length in Romans. On p 536 of the Dictionary read paragraphs (*a*) and (*b*) of Section 2, looking up all the references in Moffatt's version. This will be sufficient for present purposes; state the results as they bear on v. 56. Explain v. 57.

Read vv. 50–58 as a whole.

Compare Moffatt's version; there is no reason to think that v. 56 is a marginal note.

229

Review of 15: 35–58

(Cf. Study 8)

230

Review of Chapter 15

(Cf. Study 8)

231

In the Dictionary study the article "Resurrection," noting down the points that bear on St Paul's teaching. For further study Milligan's *The Resurrection of the Body* is a valuable standard book, but it is a little old. William Adams Brown's *The Christian Hope* is more recent, but it is small.

232

16: 1–9

Read these verses. The "collection for the saints" in v 1 was a contribution made by Gentile Christians for the benefit of the church of Jerusalem; this was a subject that interested St. Paul deeply. The theme reappears in II Corinthians 8–9 and Romans

I CORINTHIANS 15–16

15: 22–29; read these passages. The former has been termed "a classical statement of the principles of church finance"; summarize these principles briefly. The directions to the Galatians (v. 1) does not appear in our Galatians, but this Epistle refers to the theme in 2: 10.

Note carefully how St. Paul guards himself from suspicion of covetousness in vv. 2–4; was this precaution over-elaborate (Study 43)? With vv. 5–6 compare Acts 20: 1–3, and verify the references on a map.

Compare Moffatt's version. Note his interesting rendition of v. 4.

233

16: 10–24

Read these verses. Look up all the proper names in the Dictionary (together with "Maranatha"), and note down everything that bears on the interpretation of this section. v. 15 shows that the first converts of each city had a certain precedence thereafter.

With v 21 compare II Thessalonians 3: 17, Galatians 6: 11. The Epistle was written by a scribe (compare Romans 16: 22), but St Paul added a few lines at the end.

Compare Moffatt's version.

234–235

Review of Studies 206–233

(Cf Studies 31–32)

236

Review of Chapters 15-16
(Cf. Study 8)

237

Review of Sections I and II

238

Review of Sections III and IV

239

Review of Sections V and VI

240

Review of Section VII and General Review

www.ingramcontent.com/pod-product-compliance
Lightning Source LLC
Chambersburg PA
CBHW051102160426
43193CB00010B/1290